Advance Praise for

stoneview

Where else can you find working details on timber framing, cordwood masonry,
a living roof, and a floating slab foundation all in one succinct, nicely illustrated step-by-step
package? In *Stoneview*, author Rob Roy provides everything you need to build a truly sustainable
and attractive guest cottage, studio, or temporary shelter, all for under $6,000. Here's where
his 30-odd years of workshop and natural building experience really pays off,
especially for the novice builder.

— Richard Freudenberger, Publisher, *BackHome Magazine*

Stoneview is a delightfully readable and incredibly detailed account of a building project
tailor-made for those who'd like to tackle a small project before building their dream home.
It's a great introduction to natural building techniques and ideas that will prove invaluable as
you undertake other projects — written by one of the natural building world's masters.

— Dan Chiras, author of *The Natural House, The Homeowner's Guide to Renewable Energy,
The New Ecological Home, The Solar House, The Natural Plaster Book*, and many more

Rob Roy's *Stoneview* is a wonderful new addition for the natural builder's library.
Rob's extensive experience shines through in this profusely illustrated step-by-step guide for
the amateur builder. Not only an excellent introduction to cordwood building, *Stoneview* provides
a surprisingly thorough overview of a range of other systems such as frost-protected foundations,
living roofs, greywater, and using recycled materials. I am certain that this encouraging and
informative book will result in a bunch of charming little buildings popping up all over!

Joseph F. Kennedy, Director, Village Renaissance and
editor, *The Art of Natural Building,* and *Building Without Borders*

Full of common-sense ideas, *Stoneview* will let readers in on the secret of alternative
building — how great it really feels to take a project like this one to completion.
Congratulations on a job well done!

— Cliff Shockey, author of *Stackwall Construction: Doublewall Technique*

stoneview

how to build an eco-friendly little guesthouse

stoneview

how to build an eco-friendly little guesthouse

ROB ROY

NEW SOCIETY PUBLISHERS

Cataloging in Publication Data:
A catalog record for this publication is available from the National Library of Canada.

Cover design by Diane McIntosh.
Cover images by Rob Roy.

Printed in Canada.
First printing January 2008.

Paperback ISBN: 978-0-86571-597-4

Inquiries regarding requests to reprint all or part of *Stoneview* should be addressed to New Society Publishers at the address below.

To order directly from the publishers, please call toll-free (North America) 1-800-567-6772, or order online at www.newsociety.com

Any other inquiries can be directed by mail to:

New Society Publishers
P.O. Box 189, Gabriola Island, BC V0R 1X0, Canada
(250) 247-9737

New Society Publishers' mission is to publish books that contribute in fundamental ways to building an ecologically sustainable and just society, and to do so with the least possible impact on the environment, in a manner that models this vision. We are committed to doing this not just through education, but through action. This book is one step toward ending global deforestation and climate change. It is printed on acid-free paper that is 100% post-consumer recycled (**100% old growth forest-free**), processed chlorine free, and printed with vegetable-based, low-VOC inks, with covers produced using Forest Stewardship Council-certified stock. Additionally, New Society purchases carbon offsets annually, operating with a carbon-neutral footprint. For further information, or to browse our full list of books and purchase securely, visit our website at: www.newsociety.com

NEW SOCIETY PUBLISHERS   www.newsociety.com

To Bruce Kilgore and Doug Kerr, two uncommon friends.

Without Bruce, Stoneview would not be what it is today.
He provided the front door, the woodstove, the water storage
barrel and the wonderful "log-end toilet." He loaned us his cut-off
saw for the timber framing work, and helped me haul
hundreds of buckets of soil up onto the roof.

Without Doug, we would not have most of the
drawings for this book. At least, they wouldn't be as good.

In common, Bruce and Doug share an enthusiasm
for finding new solutions to problems, and continue to give
of themselves unselfishly to anyone who needs a hand.

Contents

Disclaimer

The author has shown how he (with family and friends) has built a little guesthouse using safe and sound building practices, but he does not claim that the information is complete or that the methods described will meet all building codes. Anyone wishing to use this book as a guide for building a similar structure needs to make sure that the building will pass local code. The best way to do this is to apply for a building permit and find out what is required of you. Some requirements could be different from what is advocated herein. The author and publisher have no control over how the reader chooses to use the information in this book, and we have no idea about the reader's level of competence or his or her physical conditions. Therefore, we are not responsible for mishaps or problems that occur as a result of using information in this book. The Bibliography gives good sources for additional related building information.

Acknowledgments

My sincere thanks goes to:

Chris and Judith Plant at New Society Publishers — early guests at Stoneview — for their faith in this book, sight unseen. Managing editor Ingrid Witvoet, art director Greg Green and the rest of the NSP staff for their usual fine work. And, of course, to my friend and editor, *BackHome* magazine's own Richard Freudenberger.

Neal Pressley, Dan Rivera and Tom Harris for providing pictures that they took during the Timber Framing and Cordwood Workshops at Stoneview. And to all of the other dozens of students at these workshops, too numerous to list, who helped and learned at Stoneview.

Steve Carlson for his fine line drawing of Stoneview.

Ron Sienkiewicz and all the gang at GRK Fasteners for supplying the best screws in the world for the project.

Mari Fox and Colbond Corporation for supplying the composite drainage matting for the roof.

Ed Snodgrass at Emory Knoll Farms for supplying 450 sedum plants — five different varieties — for Stoneview's living roof.

Norm Davis at Davis Sawmill for an excellent job on our Method One and Method Two posts, and for supplying the fine cedar center-post.

Friends Ronnie Marx and Steve DeLaura at Cedar Knoll Log Homes for timbers, planing, planking and several pick-up loads of cedar scraps for log-ends.

Nick Brown and Dean Koyanagi, interns extraordinaire, for their skilled help on the foundation (Nick) and the interior framing and finishing details (Dean).

Joe Young for letting me help him with the sheetrock.

Rich Douglas, Brent Wessels and Paul Washburn for help with pouring the slab. And not forgetting Touly, Plattsburgh Quarry's excellent driver.

Dan Nephew and Roger for excellent clearing and landscaping work.

Son Darin for help on the planking, waterproofing, snowblocking and assisting at workshops.

And, not least, to Jaki, my wife and partner of 35 years, for planning, photography, keeping workshops running smoothly, instruction, and more than her fair share of work of all kinds at Stoneview, but especially on the living roof.

Stoneview, indeed, has been a labor of love.

Introduction:
How Stoneview — and this Book — Came About

Spring, 2004: My book *Timber Framing for the Rest of Us* had just been published, and described timber framing using commonly available metal fasteners. I wrote the book with a view towards using it as a textbook for workshops of the same name.

Jaki and I had been teaching workshops in cordwood masonry and earth-sheltered housing for 25 years, but added a timber framing workshop in May of 2004, to see how it would fly. We needed a project of the right size for a three-day workshop. And we *always* need hands-on projects for our cordwood masonry workshops.

At the same time, I was troubled by the fact that a lot of cordwood builders seemed to gravitate towards octagonal and other polygon shapes of buildings, without paying sufficient attention to how the cordwood was going to marry up with the oddly angled corners. In fact, I'd written a chapter on the problem for *Cordwood Building: The State of the Art*. The article was theoretical, and I welcomed the chance to put theory into practice. I decided to test four different methods of doing octagon corners, all in one building. The methods would be appropriate for different people having access to different kinds of wooden members.

The next question was: What would be the purpose of the building? If we're going to spend $5,000 for a structure, we'd better have some justifiable use for it. There were two possibilities: First, we owned a 20-acre woodlot on our dirt road not far from our Earthwood Building School, a woodlot we wanted to sell. A line of thought was to build the little cabin on the property, so that the buyers would have a structure that they could begin to use immediately upon purchasing the land. They might use it as a vacation home, or as a place to live while they built a more substantial home for themselves nearby. In either case, the octagon would be a useful outbuilding (office, guesthouse, workshop, etc.) in the future.

The second possibility was to build another guesthouse at Earthwood for students and family friends to stay in. We already had two guesthouses, but they were small (100 and 125 usable square feet respectively), which limited their use to an individual or a couple, and only in the summer.

To decide which property to build on, we created lists of pros and cons for each site, which included: need, cost, convenience of building, logistical suitability as a workshop, and, oddly, some of the considerations in building in two separate townships, each having a different approach to building permits and with disparate assessment values for similar properties. Finally, we wondered if building something on the 20 acres, which we wanted to sell, would add to the value of the property and make it easier to sell, or whether we would be second-guessing the unknown buyer by putting money into something that might not be what they want. Long story short, we decided on another guesthouse at Earthwood. This turned out to be fortuitous for us and for the young couple who bought our 20 acres soon after we had made the decision. I think the added cost of the property with the guesthouse on it might have made it difficult for them to afford the place. Now, as I write two years later, I am happy to report that they are living in a charming owner-built cordwood home. And we helped them get started on their cordwood with a cordwood workshop at their place, so all came out well in the end.

There was still the question of siting the new building on our six acres at Earthwood, and this is discussed in Chapter 2. But, so that I can begin to refer to the building by its name as early as possible, I will tell you that it overlooks the largest outlier stone of our megalithic stone circle, and the new Earthwood trilithon, a work-in-progress as I write. You will see pictures of these features later in the book, and then it will become clear why we call the new guesthouse "Stoneview."

This book will be specific to building Stoneview as it is. We think it is the prettiest building we have created in the last 30 years, and visitors seem to be taken with it as well. Although we use it as a guesthouse, it would also suit as a workshop, a storage building, a garden shed or even a vacation cabin. I advocate the "temporary shelter" (TS) strategy, which I discussed in detail in *Mortgage Free!: Radical Strategies for Home Ownership* (Chelsea Green, 1994). The use of a small building like Stoneview gives the owners of the property: (1) a mortgage-free place to live while they build their dream home, (2) a project upon which to practise their building skills, (3) a useful outbuilding later on and (4) intimate familiarity with their property, a great plus in siting their home, septic system, well, access routes and outbuildings. Stoneview in particular could be a luxurious master bedroom wing (with bath) attached to the main house. My strong advice when using the TS strategy is to build the TS with mostly the same techniques and materials that you want with the dream home. Otherwise, advantage (2) above is lost. Better to make a $500 mistake on the TS than a $5,000 mistake later on the dream home.

And the book? It came about because a high percentage of people who have seen Stoneview want to know if I have plans or a book that tells how to build it. A lady neighbor of mine, when given a tour, said: "I want one of these!" So, I figured I'd better make the detailed information available.

This book is different from my others in that it is totally devoted to the construction of a specific building, with all of the various techniques described thoroughly enough so that the reader can replicate the project. My other books are subject-specific: timber framing, cordwood masonry, earth sheltering, sauna, stone circles, mortgage freedom, etc. *All the information you need to build Stoneview is in these pages.* There are simple plans herein (with measurements) and a detailed materials list. For a different design using cordwood masonry, timber-framing or earth roofs, please see my last three books from New Society on these subjects, listed in the Bibliography. They go into a lot more detail to help you to make design and construction decisions for larger or differently shaped projects.

If you build a "Stoneview" of your own, even if it doesn't overlook any stones, please send a picture or two to me at Earthwood Building School, 366 Murtagh Hill Road, West Chazy, NY 12992. If you do it in cordwood, I'll send you our Master Mortar Stuffer's certificate.

Design

The Stoneview design was predicated upon our need for a guesthouse at Earthwood that would accommodate up to four people and have a self-contained bathroom. Further, we wanted to experiment with various octagon corner methods for cordwood masonry, as well as to develop techniques for building lightweight living roofs that would be appropriate for inexperienced owner-builders.

I had 30 years of earth roof experience and knew well the importance of creating a structural plan that would carry the living roof. I also wanted to build the guesthouse at reasonable cost. Who doesn't? But, before getting into how these considerations influenced the design, I think it best that we start with …

A Short Course in the Geometry of Octagons

Back in 1967, I taught geometry at a private school in Massachusetts. That the school burned down soon thereafter is an unrelated event. After 37 years, I knew I would have to take a fresh look at the geometry of octagons if I wanted to build one. Here is a capsule look at my researches. All the important relationships required for building Stoneview are included. You really should be familiar with this stuff before embarking upon building an octagonal shaped building yourself.

First, we need a couple of simple definitions for use with this book.

5

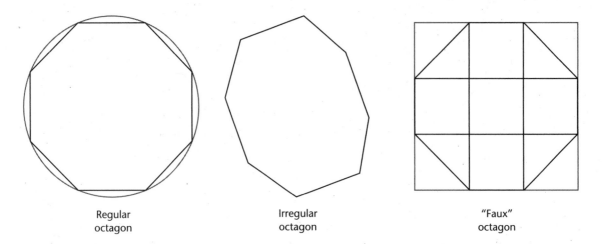

Regular
octagon

Irregular
octagon

"Faux"
octagon

Fig. 1.1: *Regular octagon.*
Irregular octagon. "Faux"
regular octagon.

Octagon. Strictly, *octagon* refers to any eight-sided closed polygon. But, for our purposes, we will consider only the "regular octagon," one where all of its sides are the same length, like a stop sign. See Figure 1.1. The center image is also an octagon, but irregular, and not of much use for our present purposes. And watch out for the octagon on the right. It looks a lot like a regular octagon, and it is easy to draw from a square grid of three squares on a side, but it yields a "faux" regular octagon; that is, the sides are not equilateral.

Radius and diameter. For our purposes, the *radius* (R) is the distance from the center of the (regular) octagon to any of its eight external points, also called the *circumradius.* Unless specified, this is the radius used in this book. However, it is useful to know of another — shorter — radius (r), called the *inradius,* which is the distance from the center (C) to the midpoint of any side (S) of a regular octagon. The long *diameter* (D) is twice the radius (R), or the distance between any two diametrically opposite points. The short diameter (d) is the width of the octagon, that is: from side to side.

To draw a regular octagon (hereinafter called, simply, an octagon) with a compass and straightedge, refer to Figures 1.2a through 1.2d and follow these instructions:

Figure 1.2a: (1) Place the pointy metal leg of a drawing compass at a selected center point C and, with the pencil leg, describe a circle of the same

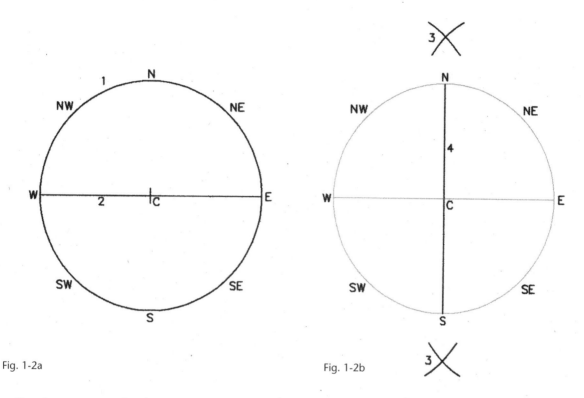

Fig. 1-2a

Fig. 1-2b

Fig. 1.2: *Seven steps to drawing a regular octagon*

radius that you want for the octagon. (2) With a straight edge, draw a horizontal line through the center of the circle so that it intersects two opposite points of the circle. This is the diameter of the octagon you want. Figure 1.2b: (3) Set the distance between the points of the compass equal to the diameter. Place the metal leg at either end of the diameter line and describe two penciled arcs, one above and one below the circle. Do the same from the point at the other end of the diameter line. (4) Place the straightedge so that it connects the two sets of intersecting arcs just created in the previous step. Within the circle, draw a line along the straightedge. This line is a second diameter at right angles to the first. You have established four points of your octagon, which we label after the four directions: N, E, S and W. Figure 1.2c: (5) Set the legs of the compass so that their tips are about a radius length apart. From each of the four directional points, describe arcs as shown in the

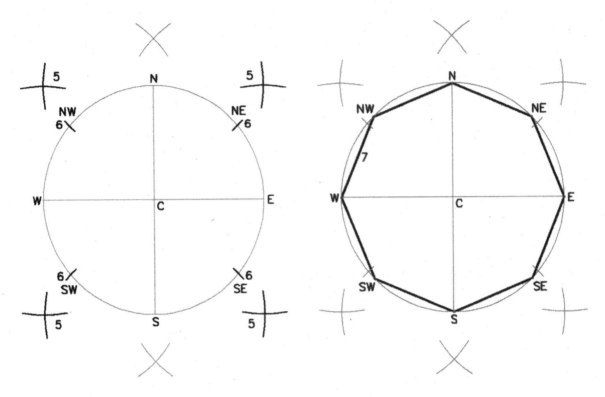

Fig. 1-2c

Fig. 1-2d

drawing, creating four new points outside of the circle. (6) Connect opposite points with two lines, creating four new intersections on the circle's circumference, labeled NE, SE, SW and NW. The directional points on the circle are the eight points of your octagon, equidistant from each other. Figure 1.2d: (7) Connect the eight points on the circle to see your newborn octagon.

Now, what if you want your octagon to be in scale? Easy. Using a convenient scale — I used ¼ inch = 1 foot — make your scaled initial radius of Step 1 above equal to the radius of the actual building. A simple example: A 24-foot diameter would be 24 divided by 4 = 6 inches on a scale drawing, or a 3-inch radius. For reasons explained in the text below, I decided on a concrete slab diameter of 21 feet 6 inches (21½ feet). This equals 5.375 inches on my scale drawing because 21.5 divided by 4 = 5.375 (5³/8). Set the radius — the distance between the metal pointed leg and the pencil point — to half the diameter, 2.687 (2¹¹/16) inches in the example.

Angles. All of the angles pertinent to an octagon are in Figure 1.3. A 45-degree angle is one of the easiest to work with. It is simply a right angle, bisected. Connecting opposite corners of a square piece of plywood, for example, yields two 45-degree angles. The 135-degree angle is simply a right angle plus a 45. It is worth purchasing a carpenter's speed square, usually made of cast aluminum, for this project. They cost about $10, and have the 45-degree angle built in. Another useful tool is the adjustable angle square (also called an angle finder), particularly useful for laying out the 135-degree angle quickly and easily.

Area. If you know the radius (R), the area of a regular octagon is found by this formula: A =2.828 x R². The area of the Stoneview slab, then, with its 10-foot 9-inch (10¾-foot) radius is found thusly: A = 2.828 x (10.75)² = 326.81

Fig. 1.3: *Useful angles in a regular octagon.*

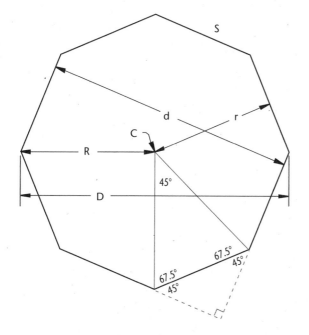

Key to letters:

C = Center.

D = "Long diameter," from any point to opposite point, the same as 2R

d = "Short diameter," of octagon measured from side to side, the same as 2r

R = "Long radius," (*circumradius*) from center to any of the eight points.

r = "Short radius," (*inradius*) from midpoint of any side to center, same as d/2

S = Length of any side

square feet. We will actually make use of this figure later when we calculate the concrete required for the slab pour. By the way, if you know the side (S), and not the radius (R), you can use a different formula for area: A = 4.8284 x S². Incidentally, the overhang of this small building has a dramatic effect on the roof area, increasing it to about 454 square feet.

Octagon dimensions. There are at least two good ways to find any dimension of an octagon if you know any other dimension. If you have Internet capability, click on the "Octagon Layout Calculator" at http://junior.apk.net/~jbarta/ octagon_layout/index.html. This wonderful free program by Joe Barta enables you to plug in any known dimension of an octagon and, instantly, it will give you all of the other dimensions in units of measure found on a standard tape measure: feet and inches. The figures are accurate to within one-sixteenth of an inch (¹/₁₆ inch). Web addresses change, so if the one cited here does not work, simply search "Octagon Layout Calculator."

Or you can use Table 1.1, below, which enables you to calculate any salient dimension of an octagon, if you know any other. The letters in the table refer to the labels of Figure 1.3.

Design Considerations for Stoneview

Please refer to the framing plan of Fig. 1.4.

We knew we wanted a living roof on the guesthouse, so we needed to keep the radius span down to something reasonable, both for cost and ease

Table 1.1

Conversion factors for a regular octagon				
If you know d:	**If you know S:**	**If you know D (2R):**	**If you know r:**	**If you know R:**
S = .414d	d = 2.414S	d = .924D	d = 2r	d = 1.847 R
D = 1.082d	D = 2.613S	S = .383D	S = .828r	S = .765 R
r = .5d	r = 1.207S	r = .462D	D = 2.167r	r = .923 R
R = .541d	R = 1.307S	R = .5D	R = 1.082r	D = 2R
(letters refer to Figure 1.3)				

of building. The large timbers that join the top of the eight posts at the top of the building's external wall are called *girts*, and they are the largest and heaviest timbers in the building, with the exception of the center post and capital assembly. Our girts would be made of 8-by-8 stock, for strength and to match the cordwood masonry's 8-inch thickness. Sawyers generally sell lumber and heavy timbers in multiples of two feet: 8, 10, 12 feet, etc. My local supplier, Cedar Knoll Log Homes in Plattsburgh, like most others, purchases its logs a few inches longer than the nominal length. Eight-footers are generally 8 feet 3 inches to 8 feet 5 inches, for example. But ten-footers would be 25 percent more expensive than eight-footers.

A second limiting factor concerned the load-bearing capacity of the sixteen 4-by-8 radial rafters that I wanted to use. I knew that I couldn't go much beyond nine feet of a clear span, even with a lightweight living roof. I went down to Cedar Knoll and selected eight white pine girts that were all at least 8 feet 4 inches or better, as I wanted a trimmed length of 8 feet 3 inches on the outer surface of the wall. (Because the top surfaces of the girts are really trapezoidal in shape, as seen from above, the inner dimension would be about 7 feet 8 inches.)

The length of the girt is the same as the length of the sidewall, labeled S in the octagon diagrams. If S is 8 feet 3 inches (8¼ feet), then the radius of the building is 1.307 times B, or 10.783 feet (10 feet 9³/8 inches).

To get as much drying as possible on the heavy timbers before using them, I hand-picked all my girts months before they would be used, and sent

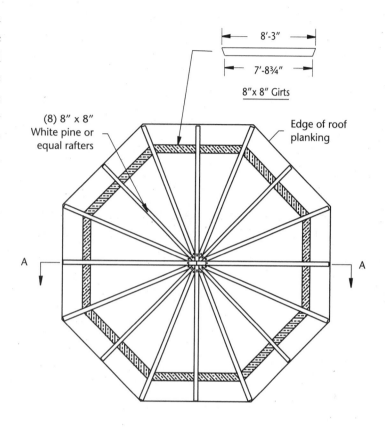

Fig. 1.4: *Framing plan for Stoneview.*

them to Cedar Knoll's planer, where they were planed on all four sides. They ended up to be 7¾ inches on each side … and very nice looking.

My plan showed me that I needed eight rafters at least 12 feet 6 inches long and eight at least 12 feet 0 inches in length. (The ones at the points are slightly longer than the ones supported halfway along the girts.) These dimensions allowed ample length for trimming and shaping both ends. In the actual event, I wound up with lots of little 6-inch scraps of four-by-eights. Cedar Knoll didn't have 4-by-8 material ready cut, but they had a good quantity of 12-foot white pine eight by eights. I selected eight good straight ones, making sure that four of them were at least 12 foot 6 inches in length. I had all eight resawn into 4-by-8 rafters and then planed on all four sides. The resulting rafters ended up with actual dimensions of 3½ by 7¾ inches, and, again, were very nice to look at.

I had all the girts and rafters delivered to Earthwood, and stacked them in neat piles with 1-by-2 wooden stickers between them so that they would season without twisting. White pine is a wood that does not suffer from twisting as it dries. When we built Earthwood, 25 years earlier, I used red pine for my 5-by-10 rafters, a mistake. Red pine often grows spirally in the forest, which will cause red pine timbers to twist as they cure.

The Octagon Posts

Eight-by-eights are an obvious post size for supporting 8-by-8 girts in a rectilinear building, such as our garage and other guesthouses. But they don't work very well with an octagon, particularly one whose sides are to be infilled with cordwood masonry. I wanted to test various methods of corner post design for an octagonal cordwood building in order to solve the problem once and for all. And what is the problem?

Figure 1.5 shows a square post with dimensions equal to the width of the cordwood wall: eight-by-eight, twelve-by-twelve, whatever. Because (1) there is no chemical bond between wood and mortar and (2) heavy timbers shrink dimensionally over time, the mortar on the exterior of the wall loosens and tends to "pop out" as shown in the diagram. On the interior, the mortar will

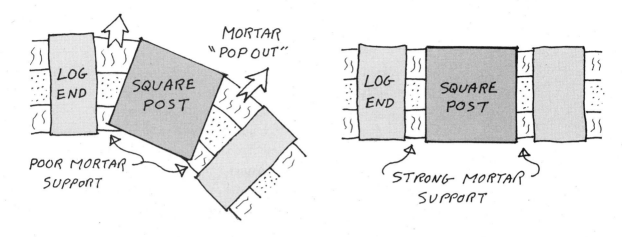

Fig. 1.5: *A square post does not work well with an octagon wall, but is great for a rectilinear building.*

not pop out, but it is difficult to get a good bearing surface against the post. With a rectilinear structure, there is no "draft angle" in the mortar cross-section to encourage the mortar to migrate outwards, and there is a nice straight bearing surface to support the mortar on the interior joint, as seen on the right-hand side of Figure 1.5. A round post is even worse, as seen in Figure 1.6.

At Stoneview, four different creative methods were used to alleviate the problem and I am pleased to report that all worked extremely well. The reader can select the one(s) that you like and/or best suits your available materials.

Norm Davis, a local sawyer, was a valuable ally in helping to create the first two methods, which I call Methods One and

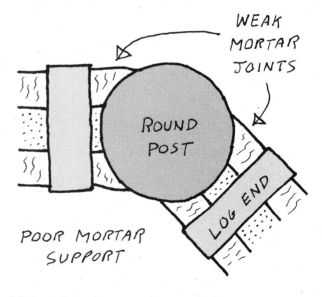

Fig. 1.6: *A round post does not provide a straight flat resistance to the cordwood masonry.*

Two. Method One is seen in Figure 1-7, and has turned out to be our favorite, visually. It involves taking a round log of sufficient diameter (about 12 inches in the case of an eight-inch-thick cordwood wall) and milling two sides as seen in the diagram. For an octagon, angle X is 45 degrees. Norm just loves this sort of challenge. It gives him a break from the regular parallel cuts he makes all day long. With Method One posts, you see the barked but unspoiled outer edge of the tree exposed, which is quite attractive. It looks a bit like a round post, but without the structural drawbacks of Figure 1.6. The key piece in the diagram will be discussed in Chapter 5 about cordwood masonry.

Method Two is very similar to Method One as to the way it works. Again, Norm did the magic at his sawmill, but this time he created the five-sided posts seen in Figure 1.8. The main differences between the methods are in appearance and in the number of cuts required to mill the posts. Method Two suggests the octagonal geometry of the building, and requires more passes through the saw. Method Two is probably a more difficult post to make, as there is more chance of an erroneous cut.

Both Method One and Method Two posts can be made at home with a beam-cutting attachment for your chainsaw. See *Timber Framing for the Rest of Us* for more information on this option and a list of tool suppliers.

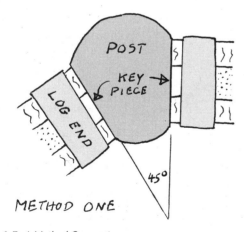

Fig. 1.7: *A Method One post.*

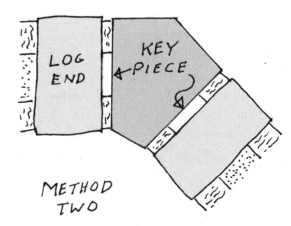

Fig. 1.8: *A Method Two post.*

Method Three (Figure 1.9) posts are appropriate if you have access to smaller logs, perhaps younger trees that you need to clear on site to make room for the building. I made two Method Three posts by marrying a three-inch-diameter log to a roughly seven-inch-diameter log, as shown. My three-incher was actually a regularly turned cedar dowel from Cedar Knoll, used for railings on their log cabins. I found it convenient to screw an ordinary finished two-by-four (actually 1½ by 3½ inches) to the seven-inch log, and then screw the three-inch dowel to the same two-by-four as shown. Later, I added the key pieces discussed in Chapter 5. The beauty of this system is that you can make use of easily available smaller logs to create the 45-degree angle needed for the octagon corners. Also, the seven-inch-diameter logs look real nice on the exterior.

Method Four (Figure 1.10) is one of these happy accidents of geometry you can take advantage of, and it is appropriate for people who have access to regular lumber. Rough-cut two-bys work particularly well. I figured it out by making a full scale plan model from cuttings of paper, matching the cross-sections of the four timbers required: two-by-two, two-by-four, two-by-six and two-by-eight.

With Method Four posts, you see the flat side of a two-by-eight on the exterior. The mind is tricked into thinking that it is an eight by eight, but it

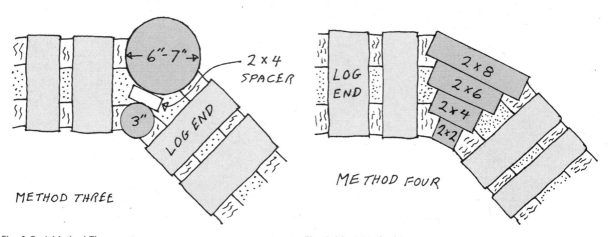

Fig. 1.9: *A Method Three post.*

Fig. 1.10: *A Method Four post.*

is not, of course, and does not have the downsides of an eight by eight. On the interior, you see a two-inch edge of the two by two. And maybe five screws used to fasten the lumber together. A side benefit of the Method Four design is the saw-tooth edges of the post where it meets the cordwood wall. These edges act as a locking key to the cordwood mortar without the need for an extra key piece.

I do not see a need for cordwood walls thicker than eight inches for such a small building, but some of my cordwood followers may want to know how to adapt these octagon post ideas to a thicker-walled building. It would take very large logs (tree trunks) to make Method One or Method Two posts for — say — a 16-inch cordwood wall. Maybe you have them (great!) ... but probably not. Method Three will work well, though, with smaller logs. Scale it out on a paper diagram for the thickness of wall you want. Finally, you may be able to adapt some variation of Method Four for your wall thickness, making use of available timbers. The idea is there; just adapt it for your situation.

The Sectional Plan

Inexperienced designer builders often neglect the important sectional drawing at the design stage. This cutaway view allows the designer to plan roof pitches, figure out stairways, and check heights of important structural elements, particularly posts in the case of Stoneview. While some buildings may require more than one sectional plan, the simple Stoneview design needs Figure 1.11 only, a section through the middle of the building, along opposing radial rafters. (This is expressed as section A-A on Figure 1.4, the framing plan.) This sectional plan gives us a look at the building's proportions and shows: the center post and capital dimensions; the 6-foot 6-inch height of the eight perimeter posts; and the roof pitch of one-in-twelve (1:12).

An elevation plan, showing the building as it looks when approached on foot, is somewhat similar to the sectional, in Stoneview's case, and could show things like window and door placement, cordwood masonry, etc. Unlike rectilinear buildings, elevation drawings are not particularly easy to

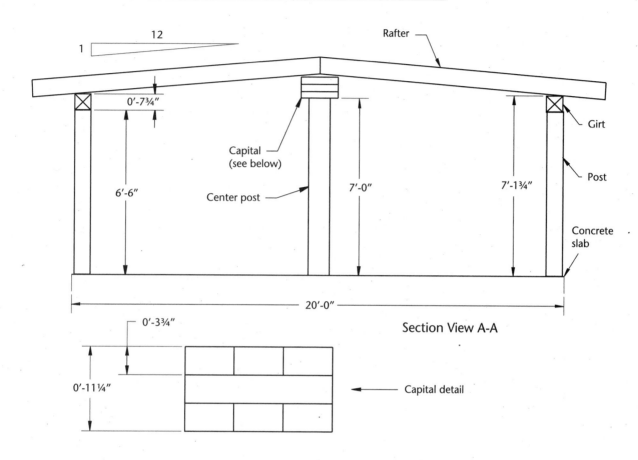

Section View A-A

Capital detail

Fig. 1.11: *A look through Stoneview's center, section A-A from Figure 1.4.*

draw for round or octagonal buildings, and are not entirely necessary for our purposes. Any exterior photo in this book shows an elevation view.

The Floor Plan

Being a thrifty kind of guy — some say cheap — I place more value on structural plans than floor plans. I want to design something easy and inexpensive to build. Many of my students bring a floor plan to consultation sessions. They may have given some thought to how to build the thing, oftentimes not. In either case, the problem is: *how to design an easy and inexpensive structure to contain the floor plan.* This approach can result in complicated and expensive structural plans. The structure already described is easy to build and makes use of inexpensive components. And it panders to people who like the octagon shape, which, incidentally, is very efficient in enclosing space with minimal skin materials. Now the problem, in my view, is quite a bit simpler: how to use the octagon for the desired purpose.

We wanted to use the space for the same purpose as a common motel room: sleeping space with a bathroom. And we wanted people to have a place to relax during times between classes and sleeping: a table and chairs, couch. And we wanted to be able to heat it with a wood stove for winter use.

Figure 1.12 is the Stoneview floor plan, as used. The only right angle is where one of the long bathroom walls meets the midpoint of one of the octagon's sides, this to provide a corner for the square shower unit.

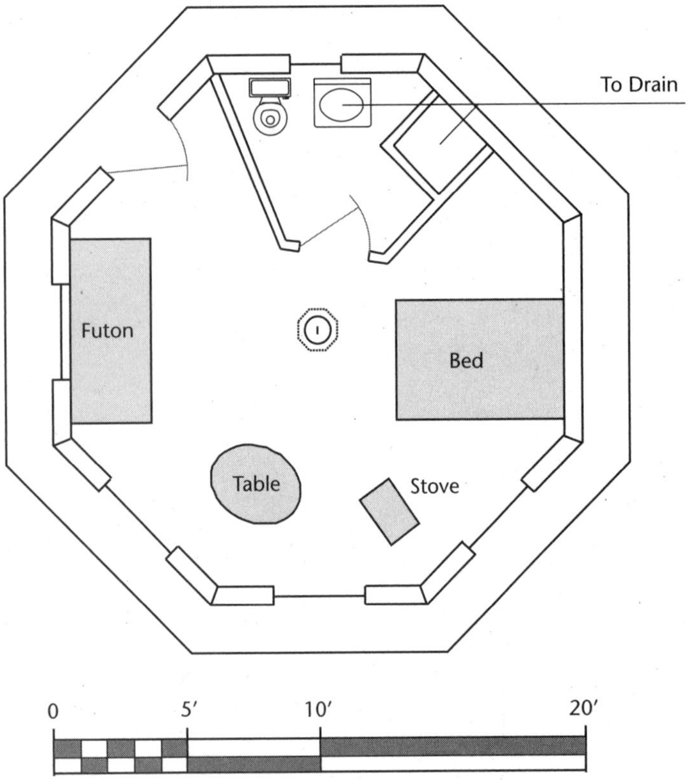

Jaki and I considered the use of two convertible futon beds, but decided in favor of a permanent double bed and a single futon that can be used for seating during the day, but can be made into a second double bed at night. We reasoned that one or two people would use the building more often than three or four, and this has proven to be the case. We designed a compact little bathroom, taking the octagon shape into consideration. We allowed space for a small woodstove and a dining table with four chairs.

Just under a fifth of the space is devoted to the bathroom, with the rest being a single room containing all of the other space uses: sleeping, relaxation, eating. There are no kitchen facilities,

Fig. 1.12: *The Stoneview floor plan.*

but there would be room for it if the building's sleeping potential does not exceed two.

Structural Design Summation

The Stoneview design evolved out of balancing space requirements, economy, and structural considerations for a living roof. I will not go into all of the thought processes, as they are redundant for someone who wants to duplicate this building. The bottom line is that the structure works, satisfies its intended purpose very nicely, is low in cost, and is structurally sound. The reader can safely duplicate the plan designs in this book in areas of 70-pound snow load or less. Just be aware that if you increase the rafter spans, you will need to have your changes checked by a qualified structural engineer. The unfortunate reality about spans is that beam strength decreases as the *square* of the span. As an example, if you start with a design with nine-foot rafter spans engineered for a particular load, and then decide to increase the span to ten feet, you might think that you would need to beef up the rafters by about ten percent. You'd be wrong. In truth, the impact of the extra foot of span is far greater. $9^2 = 81$. $10^2 = 100$. The difference, 19, must be compared to the 81: 19 divided by 81 = 23.5 percent more strength is required. I give this example as a reality check for students at my timber framing classes. Five-by-tens would certainly make up the shortfall, but the wonderful economy and ease of construction at Stoneview would both be compromised. Girts would have to come out of ten-footers, not eights. My recommendation is to follow the plan as given. Don't try to stretch the plans into a small house size. It's better to design the house you really want.

Siting and Pad Preparation

Site Selection

Fifty years ago, two acres of the six-acre Earthwood lot had been denuded of its forest and topsoil for the gravel below the surface. The gravel layer, fortunately, had a depth of about five feet, so, instead of going deeper for gravel — and creating a huge deep pit — the excavation took place laterally. This part of the land, at the top of Murtagh Hill, remained quite flat, although it had been turned into lifeless moonscape. Not a thing grew on it. Elsewhere I have told how, over the years, we have reclaimed this deadscape and turned it into living green oxygenating space. Several of the Earthwood buildings occupy this reclaimed two acres, as well as our garden, stone circle, and an entranceway and parking lot for the building school. Most of this area can be seen in Figure 2.1.

The original gravel pit was almost totally reclaimed by 2004, and there were no good building sites left on it. In fact, our other two guesthouses and associated bathhouse and screened eating area are all in the woods and accessed by our second, residential, driveway.

The stone circle, also seen in Figure 2.1, was a key component in siting the new guesthouse. In 2002, we had erected a 20-ton outlier stone to the southwest of the main circle, a stone that accurately marks the setting sun on the Shortest Day, or winter solstice, usually December 21st. See Figure 2.2. The stone is called Juliesteyna, from Jule (Yule) + steyna (Norse for a female

Fig. 2.1. *The buildings, raised bed garden, lawn, and stone circle are all reclaimed from the original gravel pit, five feet lower than the wooded area. The Stoneview site is just off-picture to the left.*

stone.) One of the features of the alignment, as seen from the viewing stone on the diametric opposite side of the circle, is a pathway that we cleared through the woods. When the sun sets at the winter solstice (and three or four days either side of it, for "solstice" means "sun stands still"), it first disappears into the forest on the south side of the cleared forest path. But the sun sets on a very low flat arc and moves as much laterally as down, so it "regleams" into the cleared way, only to set on Juliesteyna like the flame of a giant candle, as seen in Figure 2.2.

Your Siting Considerations

The Stoneview design works great on a flat site. If the subsoil is well-drained with good percolation, such as sand or gravel, all the better. If not, you can build up a pad of percolating material as explained below.

As described, the floating slab will require four cubic yards of concrete. That is not a lot, but probably more than you are going to want to mix by hand, even with a powered mixer. Therefore, it is important that a concrete truck can back up to the site on the day of the pour. In other words, you need good site access.

If you build on wooden piers, or if you decide to mix your own concrete, a much smaller access road will suffice, but you will still want to get a small pick-up truck in to carry the wooden timbers, planking, windows and door, cement, sand and other materials.

Fig. 2.2: The winter solstice sun sets over Juliesteyna. Stoneview can be seen to the right. Thus, the name.

A sloped site does not work so well for this building, at least in the form described in this book.

As for the earth roof, the best site would have some shade during part of the day. A lightweight living roof, like Stoneview's, will not do as well in constant dawn to dusk sunshine. Because of trees to the south and west, our roof gets full sun about half of the day, which seems to be perfect.

If you are planning a full septic system, make sure you have space, good percolation, and health department approval for your septic system plan. The greywater waste system described in this book does not require a septic tank or drainfield, but it is only appropriate for rural areas where you have room to compost the humanure from a composting toilet.

Finally, this is a really nice looking building, inside and out. Put it somewhere where you have a nice view looking out, and visitors have a nice view of it when walking into the site.

Clearing the Site

Our site is up on original grade, overlooking the now reclaimed gravel pit, five feet lower. The site was wooded, with a variety of large trees and small, including quite a few white birches and poplars (quaking aspen). I felled all trees in the way of the building, leaving any that had a chance of surviving construction. I cut the trees into firewood, as none of it was useful for building. Jaki and I cleared the small trees and brush to a couple of piles in the woods, which provide habitat for small wildlife. Some of it was broken up into dry kindling wood a year later.

This rough clearing took us down to the topsoil layer, punctured by a couple of dozen stumps, from three inches up to about six inches in diameter. That's when we brought in our contractor friend, Dan Nephew, with his heavy backhoe. I'd worked with Dan and his operator, Roger, on other projects and they both had a good sense of what I wanted done and the best way to do it. Part of this comes from giving good, clear and complete instructions as to what it is you are looking for, particularly if you are doing something a little out of the ordinary, such as creating a round sand pad.

Roger pulled all of the larger stumps with the bucket of the backhoe, shook them for their valuable topsoil — the stuff in the root system is particularly rich — and deposited them in the woods, becoming "Habitat for Animality." He put smaller stumps next to the edge of the drop-off formed many years earlier when the gravel pit was excavated.

Next, with his big loader bucket, Roger scraped the topsoil down to the subsoil, and pushed some of this topsoil over the buried small stumps, creating a gentle slope where there used to be a fairly severe drop-off. Later, we grassed this area, which makes a very nice approach to the rear of the building. Directly to the east of the building site was a rock garden that Jaki and I had built from the several cubic yards of material that came out of Juliesteyna's immense socket hole. The rest of the topsoil was pushed aside for later use in landscaping around the building.

Now we had a fairly flat round cleared area of about 30 feet in diameter. Stoneview's foundation footprint was an octagon about 22 feet across at the points (actually 21 feet 6¾ inches.)

The Sand Pad

I have had excellent success over the years by using Frank Lloyd Wright's favorite foundation system for frost protection: the floating slab. Frost heaving (which causes structural damage) occurs when water freezes and expands. The uplifting can cause damage to floor joists, roof rafters and other structural members. Wright reckoned (and I liberally paraphrase): "No water, no freezing. No freezing, no heaving."

The key to the floating slab (also known as the *Alaskan slab* or the *slab-on-grade* is the pad of percolating material upon which the slab "floats." Floating, in this sense, means that any expansion — or settling — that takes place will happen to the same degree anywhere on the slab. Expansion is not likely anyway, because the percolating pad carries underslab water away to some point downgrade. Settling, if any, will not be differential because every square foot of the pad is installed in the same way, as discussed below.

While crushed stone and gravel (mixed sand and stone) will work fine as pad material, I prefer to make my pad of coarse sand. Sand is easier to rake, to shovel, to compact, and to sculpt with a hoe or other hand tools. Coarse sand is preferable to fine sand, because it has a better "percolation rate." Simply stated, it drains water away better and faster.

After Roger had created a roughly 30-foot-diameter area down to undisturbed earth, we brought in a tandem dumper load of sand, about 12½ cubic yards. Roger backed the big truck up to the slope and gunned it, getting almost to the top of the slope that surrounded the old gravel pit surface. I was impressed. He dumped the whole load at or near the top of the slope, where it was easy to spread with the loader of his backhoe. A bulldozer would have been nice for this job, but the project was small enough that Roger was able to make fairly quick work of spreading the sand with the loader bucket. After, there was a uniform thickness over the whole area of about six inches. I had him drive over the pad a number of times with the backhoe, and then Roger went down the Hill for a second tandem load of sand.

While he was gone, I compacted the damp sand with a powered compactor hired at the Rent-All store. A little more than half of the second load was deposited near the top of the slope again, and the rest of the load stored at the bottom of the slope for use as needed to complete the pad. Again, Roger spread the sand and drove over it. Again I pounded the material with the compactor. My pattern is to compact north and south, then east and west, and, finally, in a clockwise spiral, so that every square foot gets hit three times. See Figure 2.3.

Final leveling was done by hand with additional material from below, until I had a good honest foot of compacted sand over the 30-foot-diameter circle. The pad was complete, with its outer skirt, about three feet wide, sloped away from the flat central 24-foot-diameter core. This flat core is sufficient to carve our 21-foot 6¾-inch diameter octagon slab out of the sand, even allowing an inch of insulation and the 2-inch thickness of the footing forms.

I found the center by trial and error, measuring off a movable block of wood to the various outside edges of the sand pad. Then I replaced the block

with a central stake pounded firmly into the pad. A finishing nail in the center of the stake gave me a place to clip my tape measure, making it easier to find the perimeter of the octagon.

Consider Figure 3.2, the footing plan, in Chapter 3. The easiest way to lay out an octagon is by subtending a circle of the same diameter, as detailed in Chapter 1, Figure 1-2. As we wanted a roughly 22-foot diameter octagon, I described a 22-foot diameter circle in the sand. Next, I had to decide the approximate locations for the eight posts; that is: how the octagon will be orientated. Here, the reader building his or her own version may like to consider where true south is, in order to maximize solar gain for winter heating. But,

Fig. 2.3: *The author compacts the sand pad with a hired power compactor.*

with an octagon, this probably won't make a great deal of difference. For me, a more important consideration was the location of some trees that I wanted to save. I tried to place the octagon points between trees, being cognizant of the 22-inch roof overhang as well, so that the trees would not brush the completed building.

I placed a log-end at the most significant of the eight external points in the octagon (with respect to trees), 12 feet from the center. Next, I placed another log-end at the point on the opposite side. Let's call this the east-west diagonal. Next, I placed two more log-ends 12 feet from the center along an estimated north-south axis. By measuring from the existing points at east and west, I can zero in the north and south points quite accurately. Similarly, I found the other four points (NE, SE, SW and NW) and marked them with log-ends. After a while, I was happy that the octagon was pretty much centered in my sand pad — having roughly the same size of skirt all around the building — and I was satisfied with how the orientation worked out with the trees I wanted to save. A little handwork was necessary with shovel, wheelbarrow, rake and hand tamper, but that is to be expected. I had plenty of sand in reserve in the smaller pile left over from the second truckload.

Slab Drainage

Remember that the principle of the floating slab is to get rid of the water under the foundation. Sand is good drainage material, and the coarser the sand, the better. The sand I got from Dan was finer than I would have liked, but I decided to go with it. To be on the safe side, I decided to improve the underslab drainage by incorporating four-inch perforated drain tubing in the sand pad, as seen in Figure 2.4. This inexpensive drainage tubing has lots of little slits cut into it, allowing water to enter into the tube, which carries it away. With a hoe, we make a track for the tube in the sand pad and slightly slope the tubing from its high point in the north to the T-junction on the south side of the circle. At the T, I changed to non-perforated pipe, which continues slightly down to a point in a retaining wall below, where it comes out above grade. The circle of perforated tubing is placed such that no part

of the sand pad is more than about six feet from the drain. Any water in the slab, then, is drained away rapidly "to daylight." I'd still use the perforated tubing with good coarse sand. It's cheap insurance. Cover the daylight end with a rodent proof ¼-inch grid metal mesh, or you might be creating a chipmunk condominium under your building.

Fig. 2.4: A four-inch perforated drain carries any water in the pad to daylight. Note the log-ends temporarily marking the corners of the octagon.

Planning the Footing Forms

With a small building like Stoneview, it makes sense to pour the footings and the floor at the same time, the so-called "thickened edge floating slab." With large buildings, like Earthwood, I like to pour the footings one day and — using the footings as screed guides — pour the floor on a different day. As we would do both jobs at once at Stoneview, I needed to have a clear idea of relative elevations for the footings and the floor. Incidentally, an advantage of pouring monolithically in this way is that only half as much forming material is required, as will be seen.

The top of the leveled pad would be the base for the floor insulation (an inch of Dow Styrofoam®) and the concrete floor slab above it. We always regretted not having put this insulation at our round cordwood cottage at Chateaugay Lake, and Jaki insisted upon it at Stoneview, so that the guesthouse could be used in the winter. Without the insulation, it would take a lot more energy to heat the slab.

With in-floor radiant heating, slabs are generally four to six inches in thickness, but we would heat this small building with a woodstove, so we were aiming for a nominal four-inch-thick slab, knowing that a good honest three inches would be plenty. A footing thickness of eight inches is sufficient for this building, even with its post-and-beam frame, eight inches of cordwood masonry infilling, and the living roof. Even Earthwood, with 16-inch-thick walls and a much heavier earth roof, stands quite happily on nine-inch-thick (by 24 inch-wide) footings.

A footing width of 12 inches is appropriate for a small building like this. Again, we wanted to run our extruded polystyrene insulation right around the footings, to prevent direct conduction to the exterior, the so-called "energy nosebleed." So, what we ended up with for a thickened edge footing detail was a cross-section that looked like Figure 3.1 in Chapter 3. With hoe, rake, shovel and tamper, it was an easy matter to carve away enough of the compacted sand to have a sculpted

Fig. 2.5: Intern Nick Brown tamps the inner edge of the thickened edge footing track.

trough as seen in the illustration, with enough room for the Styrofoam®, and the footing forms themselves. See Figure 2.5.

The Soakaway

We're going to cover forming and pouring the floating slab in Chapter 3, but, if you want waste plumbing under the slab, now is the time to do it, before the footing forms are installed.

Stoneview's plumbing consists of a simple composting system, as per Joe Jenkins' *The Humanure Handbook* (see Bibliography), and a soakaway pit for the greywater from the wash-hand basin and the shower. There is no kitchen sink in the building, although one could easily be included if desired. The simple plumbing system is further described in Chapter 8, but, for the moment, it is important to describe the installation of the drainpipes from the sink and shower to the soakaway, before the concrete is poured.

Eight feet from the northwest side of the building, we dug a pit about four feet deep and three feet in diameter, as well as a track for the two-inch PVC plastic drainage plumbing. I have shown the location of the soakaway and the plumbing on the floorplan, Figure 1.12. The soakaway pit was filled to within ten inches of grade with grapefruit-sized rocks from the old stone wall nearby. The stones were then covered with #2 (1-inch) crushed stone, three inches of hay flakes as a filtration mat, and, finally, with topsoil, seed and mulch.

Waste Plumbing in the Sand Pad

I purchased all my plumbing parts and laid them out on the ground as seen in the plan. Note that the basin drain line connects to the main house drain by way of a Y-branch fitting. Then, by hand, I dug tracks in the sand pad to take the wastewater plumbing to the soakaway pit. The Y-connector is close to the footing track, but just below the bottom of that track. Run the plumbing under concrete, not through it (which would weaken the slab.) It is easiest to install the plumbing after the footing tracks are carved, but before the forming boards are placed.

The proper slope for horizontal waste lines is ¼-inch of drop per foot of run, which translates to an inch of drop along a four-foot level. Once your plumbing mock-up fits the tracks, and with the proper slope, you can make the joins permanent with the appropriate glue for the type of plastic pipe you have selected. Use a pencil to benchmark two adjacent components to be joined, such as an elbow or Y, and the pipe. Then, etch the pipe with etching fluid made for the purpose, and glue the join according to instructions on the can of glue. Lay the whole assembly in the track and tamp damp sand around it for support.

At this time, you can also fit the two-inch vertical pipe from the bathroom wash-hand basin and the vertical pipe that will eventually connect to the shower drain, but don't permanently glue them to the waste line just yet. It is too easy for them to get bumped during the footings prep. And the shower connection should not be glued in any case until you are ready to actually install the shower base itself. What to do about the shower connection is best covered in the next chapter about preparing for the pour, as there is a nice illustration there to help.

Test your simple plumbing system by actually pouring water in both the basin drainpipe and the shower drainpipe, and make sure that the water finds its way easily to the soakaway. To keep sand and kids' small toys out of the plumbing, cover the openings with two-inch termination caps made for the purpose, or use a sturdy homemade equivalent, such as plenty of duct tape.

We've discussed siting, the sand pad (including the thickened edge footing tracks) and underslab plumbing in this chapter. That's enough. We'll cover the rest of the preparation for the slab pour, and the pour itself, in the next chapter.

The Slab

Making and Placing the Footing Forms

A good strategy for keeping building costs down, on any project, is: "Make use of what you've got." In that spirit, we used some full-sized ten-foot 2-by-6 planks for our forming boards that I had purchased at low cost a few years earlier. Two-by-eights would have been ideal, but, if one is careful during the pour, the two-by-sixes work fine. The Styrofoam® helps, as seen in Figure 3.1.

From the slab and footings plan, Figure 3.2, the eight sides of the planned concrete slab are each 8 feet 3 inches in length. But, as we are going to insert an inch of Styrofoam® between the concrete and the footing forms, and each octagon side, S, gets longer as it gets further from the center, the inner dimensions of the footing forms really need to be 8 feet 4¼ inches. I cut the ends of my ten-foot two-by-sixes at an angle as shown in Figure 2.5 in Chapter 2 so that their inner dimensions were 8 feet 4¼ inches and their ends butted up against each other. I used some mending plates (sometimes called "truss plates") to join the eight footing forms to each other around the octagonal ring. One can be seen in Figure 5.12. These 4 by 6-inch galvanized metal plates have hundreds of little spikes sticking out of them. They are easily bent to the 135-degree exterior angle found at each of the eight points of an octagon. Later, after the pour, they are fairly easily removed. (Keep them, as they will be handy later on to serve a similar purpose on the roof's retaining timbers.)

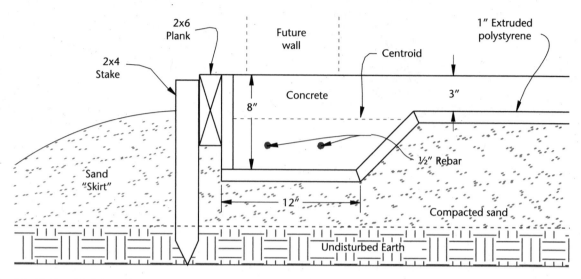

Fig. 3.1: *Footing detail, in section.*

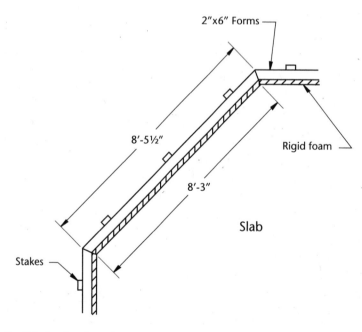

Fig. 3.2: *Footing dimensions.*

To assure a flat and level slab, it is important that the tops of all the footing forms be at the same elevation. The best way to do this is to use a strong center stake firmly driven into the sand pad. You can see my center stake, a sharpened cedar log, in Figure 3.3. Then, with a long straightedge and a four-foot level, we set all the tops of the footing forms at the same grade. For a straightedge, I used my trusty old screed board, a straight 12-foot rough-cut two-by-eight. I would span from the center to the forming boards, raising or lowering the boards as necessary. This is a good two-person job. Drive three 2-by-2 or 2-by-4 wooden stakes into the ground on the outer edge of each

forming board — one in the middle, one each about two feet from the ends. Then, when you've got the top elevation just right, make it fast by coming through the stake with a 3½-inch screw and into the forming board. Screws allow for easy form removal after the pour and are more forgiving if you have to make a correction.

Fig. 3.3: With a hoe, the author sculpts the thickened center column support. Note center stake, used for measuring and leveling the footing forms.

Insulating the Slab ...

... is optional, and probably unnecessary in southern climes. But, in the north, we wanted to maintain the option of heating the building in the wintertime, so the insulation was important. I managed to find a pretty good deal on 1-inch by 2-by-8-foot sheets of Dow Styrofoam Blueboard®, an excellent choice for below grade applications, because it has high compression strength (won't crush under the load) and it is "close-celled" (doesn't absorb water in good drainage situations.) I felt that an inch of extruded polystryrene, with an insulation value of R-5, was adequate for a small guesthouse like Stoneview.

Installing the Styrofoam® was as almost as easy as laying it out on the smooth tamped sand pad. *Almost.* The first dozen sheets went down real fast, then we had to cut sheets to fit. This is not a big problem with the octagon design, as an angle cut made on a sheet will usually yield a useful scrap for the opposite corner. You will soon work out an efficient pattern. You can see what we did in Figures 3.4 and 3.5. Note that we cut a circle of Styrofoam® out of the centermost two sheets, and used the cutout pieces under the thickened

Fig. 3.4: *We covered the bottom of the footings portion of the thickened edge slab with foot-wide pieces of 1-inch Styrofoam® brand extruded polystyrene.*

central pillar footing. In all, we used about 27 sheets (432 square feet) of 1-inch by 2-by-8-foot Styrofoam® sheets to cover the floor and the footings portion of the slab, including the outer edges of the footing trough. We held the tough but lightweight sheets in place with rocks from a nearby stonewall until we were ready to pour.

I placed 12-inch wide strips on the bottom of the footing tracks, seen in Figure 3.1 and Figure 3.4. Above this foot-wide piece, I cut and placed eight-inch strips of Styrofoam® against the footing forms. Another strip of Styrofoam® was placed at an angle to cover the sloped part of the footing track. This can be seen in Figure 3.1 and Figure 3.5.

Fig. 3.5: *We started with 8½ sheets of insulation along the north-south axis, then placed other sheets to the east and west of those, finally fitting the other four "corners" of the octagon with cut sheets.*

The alert reader may notice that the upright parts of the plumbing pipe do not show in Figure 3.5. We temporarily covered the underslab plumbing with two-inch plastic end caps made for the purpose, and laid out the Styrofoam® unimpeded. Later, on the day of the pour, I glued and installed the upright drainpipe for the wash-hand basin, leaving it extending a foot or so above the slab, and capped again for protection. Also, just under the Styrofoam® is:

The Box for the Shower Connection

A plumber taught me a trick many years ago that has held me in good stead every time I have used it. It is a trick to thwart the designs of the mischievous Mr. Murphy, famous for his Murphy's Law: "If it can go wrong, it will." In this case, the chances of placing the two-inch elbow in exactly the right place to receive the shower base unit is slim to nil. Therefore: Install a roughly 18-inch square "box" made of 2-by-4 material, such that the top of the box is at the same level as the top of the footing forms. This box can be seen a little further on in Figure 3.10, taken during the pour itself. Have a peek at it now, if you like. To make my box, I cut two scraps of two-by-four at 14 inches and two at 18 inches and nailed them so that inner dimensions of my box are 14 by 14 inches and the outer dimensions are 18 by 18 inches. I let my waste plumbing line run a little longer than the middle of the boxed area and left the pipe loose enough that it could be swung a couple of inches right and left. This way, I can do my final cutting, fitting of the two-inch elbow, and gluing just before I actually install the shower base itself. Months later — for we were in no hurry — the old plumber's trick worked perfectly once again. There was enough flexibility in the pipe, and space in the box to work, that I got my drain in just the right place (center of the shower base) and at the right elevation. With a sledgehammer, I tamped damp sand all around the pipe and elbow to keep it in place.

Reinforcing Bar ...

... is also known in different areas as rebar, rerod and resteel. For the Stoneview project, ten-foot lengths of half-inch (½-inch or #4) rebar worked perfectly, two along each of the eight sides, as per Figure 3.1. Superimpose the rebar over the footing tracks, as best you can. No, they don't fit, because they are about two feet too long. Not to worry. With chalk or tape, mark the location where you would like to bend the rebar to a 135-degree angle, so that it will fit nicely in the track, as seen in Figure 3.6. The two pieces, which will be installed about six inches apart from each other, will not be bent the same, as the pieces closer to the center of the building have a slightly shorter straight portion than the outer piece. This is why we lay them out and mark them.

Fig. 3.6: *Two pieces of ½-inch rebar run around the footing tracks, as per text.*

Note that the rebar is supported by clean broken bricks, each about three inches thick and spaced three or four feet apart. These bricks become a part of the concrete and hold the rebar three inches off the bottom of the pour. This way the rebar is correctly placed in the lower half of the pour, where it is in tension. This tensile strength on the bottom of what is essentially a grade beam, resists differential settling. If placed in the top of the form, or at the centroid (neutral axis), the rebar does not perform its intended task. Broken bits of clean flat stone, 2½ to 3 inches in thickness, will do the same job. You can also purchase wire or plastic "chairs" or "frogs" to hold the rebar in place. But I have never used them.

We also take care in keeping the rebar at least 2½ inches from any edge of the footing track, again for strength considerations.

Bending half-inch rebar is not difficult, particularly if you have a megalithic wall handy, as we have at Earthwood. I simply insert the rebar (up to its chalk mark) between two extremely heavy stones — 500-pounders or better — and lift up with the long end. The great leverage makes bending the steel very easy. You may need to come up with a different sort of creative mechanical advantage, such as holding the rebar down to the ground beneath a car or truck wheel.

At the octagon corners, each piece of rebar laps the next one by about 20 to 24 inches, satisfying the rule of overlapping rebar by forty times (40X) its diameter. Forty times a half-inch is 20 inches. The overlapping pieces are wired to each other with forming wire, twisted around adjacent pieces with a pair of pliers.

Reinforcing the Concrete Floor

The floor portion of the thickened edge slab needs to be reinforced, as well. In years past, I would use wire mesh for the purpose, but, lately, I have switched to using ready-mix concrete having the reinforcing included, in the form of millions of polypropylene fibers added to the mix at the batch plant. The fibers accomplish the same purpose as the mesh, which is to hold the concrete together when and if it cracks. With no protection, concrete can separate or lift along a crack line. The reality of concrete is that, despite all your best efforts, shrinkage or stress cracks are likely. I have rarely, if ever, seen a slab without a crack. But, with reinforcing, minor cracks are not a problem. The fibers only add about $8 per cubic yard to the cost, and their use is cheaper and easier than the wire mesh option.

Speaking of concrete, it is time to figure out how much is needed, as I can think of no other preparations required before pouring.

Calculating the Concrete Quantity

There are different ways of breaking down the volume of the thickened-edge floating slab. I'm going to share how I did it, with the actual numbers, as it worked well for us.

We're working with a thickened-edge octagon here, so let's start with the entire area of the slab and calculate the volume as if the entire octagon was as thick as the average depth of the footings. We will need accurate footing-depth measurements to make this work. I took all my measurements after the Styrofoam® was installed, but always stood on the foam, pressing it to the sand, in order to get accurate measurements.

The area of an octagon is 2.8284 times r², where r is the radius from the center to any of the eight points. From actual field measurements, I used a radius of 10.94 feet (the average distance from the center to each of the eight points). So the area of the slab would be: 2.83 x 10.94 x 10.94 = 338.63

square feet. Now that we have the area, we can get the volume of concrete to order by using four logical steps:

(Step 1) Let's start with the volume of a "superslab" that is fully as thick as the footings are deep. To do this, we multiply its area times the average depth of the footings, and the accuracy of this depth measurement is critical. The volume equals the area times the height (or depth) of the slab. (V = A x h). A slight error on *h* can have a huge impact. For example: if, in Step 2 below, we capriciously estimate a depth measurement (h) of 3 inches (.25 feet) for the non-thickened edge portion (the floor) and the actual floor thickness is 4 inches (.33 feet), we will be about a third short, or about a cubic yard in this case. A half-inch error translates to a half cubic yard. So, although I am using the actual numbers from Stoneview here, I am taking care to tell you how to calculate this yourself, because your numbers and concrete volume will be different than ours, possibly by a half cubic yard or more. A half cubic yard extra is a lot of concrete to get rid of, but even worse is running a half — or even a quarter — of a cubic yard short.

To get depth measurements (for both footings and floor), I ran a long straightedge (my screed board) from the center stake to the tops of the footing forms. Then, while standing on the insulation in the bottom of the footing track, I measured down to the insulation with a ruler, and noted the footing depth on a notepad. I'd take two depth samples in each footing track, about a quarter of the way, and three-quarters of the way, along the side. I'd work to the nearest one-sixteenth of an inch: 8¼ inches, 7⁷/₈ inches, 8⁵/₁₆ inches, etc. Adding the sixteen numbers gave me a total of 135.5 inches. Dividing by the 16 samples taken gives me an average depth of 8.47 inches. I want to work in feet, so I divide this number, 8.47, by 12 (because there are 12 inches in a foot) which results in a depth of .706 feet.

Area times height equals volume, so: 338.63 square feet times .706 feet equals almost exactly 239 cubic feet. I keep all volume measurements in cubic feet, until the very last step, Step 4. Remember that this is the volume of the octagon if you were pouring the whole thing at the depth of the footings. But we're not, so:

(Step 2) We need to know the volume of the sand pad and Styrofoam® under the floor portion, the part of the 239 cubic feet in Step 1 which will *not* be concrete. We need a new radius and a new set of depth measurements. For the radius, I measured from the center to a point above the middle of the chamfered slope, seen in Figure 3.1 and Figure 3.5. This yields a good average radius for the floor portion. From measurements (and my old notes), I see that this radius is 9.9 feet. Again, an octagon's area = 2.83 times r^2, so: 2.83 x $(9.9)^2$ = 277.21 square feet. To get depth measurements (really critical here, as we have seen), I took 24 measurements in the locations shown in Figure 3.7. The total of these measurements, mostly between $2^{5/8}$ inches and $3^{1/8}$ inches, came to 66.75 inches. Dividing by the 24 samples yields an average depth of 2.78 inches. Converting to feet: 2.78 inches divided by 12 inches per foot gives and average floor slab depth of .232 feet. Aren't pocket calculators wonderful?

Now, from Step 1, we know that the total depth of an octagon as deep as the footings is .706 feet. By subtracting the concrete floor depth (.232 feet) from this total depth (.706), we can deduce that the difference — .474 feet — represents the volume of sand pad and Styrofoam® which will *not* get poured in concrete. This volume is 277.21 square feet times .474 foot, or 131.4 cubic feet. This figure needs to come off of the 239 cubic feet from Step 1. So: 239 cubic feet minus 131.4 cubic feet leaves 107.6 cubic feet. Now, there is just one more slight adjustment to make, an addition this time.

(Step 3) Under the center-post location, I thickened the floor pour to about eight inches over a diameter of about two feet. You can see this clearly back in Figure 3.3 and Figure 3.5. From the volume of a cylinder ($V = \pi r^2 h$), I can determine that this thickened central pillar footing is going to add 1.3 cubic feet back into the

Fig. 3.7: We took 24 depth measurements at the locations shown.

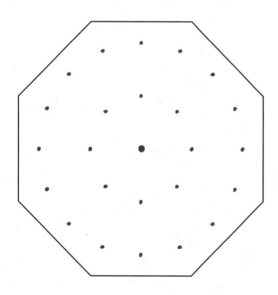

total. So: 107.6 cubic feet (from Step 2) plus 1.3 cubic feet (extra concrete under the central post) equals 108.9 cubic feet required.

(Step 4) This is the easy step. We work in feet, square feet and cubic feet, for convenience. But we buy concrete by the cubic yard. As there are 27 cubic feet in a cubic yard, all we need to do is to divide cubic feet by 27 to get our concrete order: 108.9 cubic feet divided by 27 cubic feet to the cubic yard equals 4.033 cubic yards. Well, that is so darned close to four cubic yards that it isn't funny, so that is what I ordered. I was always careful to err in my measurements on the high side, so I figured I was safe. Plus, I prepared at least a couple of cubic feet of clean washed stones to put in the center of the building in case I ran a little short. Finally, I had four bags of Sakrete® (about 2.4 cubic feet total) at the ready just in case, left over from a previous project. Sakrete® is an excellent dry mix of sand, pea gravel and Portland cement which can be made into very nice concrete by mixing it in a wheelbarrow. You get about 0.6 cubic feet per 80-pound bag.

The Crew and the Concrete

Assemble a good work crew ahead of time, so that the pour will go smoothly. We had intern Nick Brown staying with us, an excellent worker. In addition, a contractor friend, Rich Douglas, came by with his experience, as well as Brent Wessels (who was planning a similar project for himself and wanted the experience) and neighbor Paul Washburn. Jaki was there, too, and did all the photography, and much more. I couldn't have asked for a better crew, even though some of them had never poured concrete before. In reality, we would have been fine with one person less — it is a small pour — but many hands made for light work, and the job went quickly and smoothly.

On the day before the pour, I arranged with our local concrete batch plant for an 11 a.m. delivery and made sure that my helpers would be there ahead of time. I ordered four cubic yards of 3,000 psi test concrete, with the reinforcing fibers included. My receipt of May 25, 2004, shows a total cost for concrete of $320. The $80 per yard included $8 per yard for the "fiber mesh." State sales tax added $23.30. The price of concrete normally includes delivery, unless you are beyond a certain distance from the plant. I checked to make sure that there would be no "small load charge" for just four cubic yards. There was not, but this is something you might want to ask about.

The truck arrived on time and was able to back right up the slope to the pour. Figure 3.8.

The Pour

The final adding of water and mixing should take place at the site. You want to ask the driver for a "four-inch slump" to get the full strength. This is fairly stiff concrete, but that's the only way to get the full strength mix that you are paying for. Avoid the temptation of pouring soupy concrete. Sure, it

Fig. 3.8: The truck backed right up the hill to the edge of the pour. Note the quantity of slates spread on the grass and the picnic table. These have had Acryl-60® bonding agent applied to the side of the slate that will be set into the concrete (described later.)

makes the work go fast and easy, but you will not have the strength and there will be more cracking as all that water transpires out of the slab during the cure.

Arm a couple of the crew with heavy metal-tined ground rakes for pulling concrete, and have a couple of long-handled spades available for throwing extra where needed. As this was a small pour, and the chutes could reach any part of it, it didn't matter where we started. For convenience, we began by pouring the thickened center portion, holding a huge block of wood in place there, a replacement for the cedar center stake. This block of wood was carefully made and set so that its top edge surface was the same as the tops of the footing forms. We would screed off this block, but it was easily removable

Fig. 3.9: *We poured the center first, then started in on the north side.*

Fig. 3.10 and 3.11: *Two views of the screeding process. Paul, at the center, moves the screed board back and forth over a large center block resting on the Styrofoam®, while Rich works from the outside. With a rake, Nick draws extra concrete away from the leading edge of the board, so that we can keep moving forward easily.*

later on. Next, we began to pour concrete on the northern side of the footing track, being careful not to dislodge the rebar from its brick supports. Over the next 45 minutes, we worked our way back towards the truck, removing chutes as needed. Figure 3.9. The driver has lots of experience — he does this every day — so use him as a valuable resource. He — or she — will keep you right, but all responsibility for the pour is still yours.

To prevent voids around the edge, use rakes, hoes or other tools to vibrate the concrete up against the footing forms.

Finishing the Surface

It wasn't long before two of our crew needed to start the screeding process. Using a long stout straight-edge — my old 2-by-8 screed board with handles — two people flatten the concrete by drawing the board back and forth, always pushing extra concrete forward of the bottom edge of the board. See Figure 3.10 and Figure 3.11. Extra concrete is drawn away with rakes. Someone with a shovel can place extra concrete to fill voids. The board can be lifted, brought back a few feet, and the area rescreeded.

Fig. 3.12: *Bull-floating the slab.*

Where a smoothly finished floor is required, two more processes complete the job: bull-floating and power troweling.

Bull-floating is drawing a large 8- by 36-inch (typically) magnesium or aluminum float over the concrete after it has been screeded. This further smoothens and flattens the concrete and brings water and fines up to the surface, for use during the troweling process. Extension handles allow this process to take place from outside the perimeter of the pour.

You can hand-trowel or power-trowel the surface. For a very smooth floor, use a power trowel, and find someone used to operating it if you are inexperienced. This gas-powered tool has four rotating trowel blades that produce a very glassy surface. You can hire both the bull-float and the power trowel at equipment rental stores. We did not use these tools, for reasons explained in

Fig. 3.13: *The power trowel.*

the next part, but I include views (Figures 3.12 and 3.13) of their use at a neighbor's basement floor project, as the reader may prefer a smoothly finished floor.

To complete the pour, we pulled the large wooden block out of the center and filled that with concrete. The driver said we were just about out of concrete, so I threw a few clean washed stones in the center with the concrete and vibrated them in. We ended up with about enough concrete left over to make a single tier of a 12-inch layer cake. Everyone was impressed. With the great crew we had on hand, the pour was completed in about 45 minutes. Brent, Paul and Rich left and Jaki, Nick and I began hand-troweling the first parts that we poured. There was no hurry, as the concrete was not setting all that fast.

Roofing Slates as Floor Tiles

Jaki and I decided to employ a floor technique that we used successfully at the other two guesthouses: setting roofing slates directly into the freshly poured concrete. At the Earthwood house, roofing slates have been installed throughout the lower story for well over 20 years, and with no sign of wear. A friend donated 56 full-sized (10- by 14-inch) slates to the project, recycled from his neighbor's roof ... and loaned us a slate cutter! We decided to use the slates to highlight Stoneview's octagonal geometry: eight "spokes" of seven slates each, heading from the points of the octagon to within about 18 inches of the center, where there would be a post.

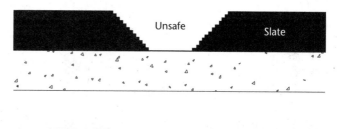

We selected the strongest slates for this use, which are, in general, a quarter inch thick or better. We rejected thin flimsy ones. The former top side of the slate will become the side that is set into the concrete, so that the rough edge is hidden into the concrete, as seen in Figure 3.14.

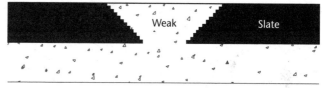

The slates are cleaned with water and a nylon brush, and then, on the morning of the pour, the side of the slate to be set into the concrete is coated with Acryl-60®, DAP or similar bonding agent and laid out to dry as per Figure 3.8. Make a few extra for breakage and rejects. Use a brush or roller to quickly apply the bonding agent.

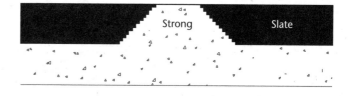

We did not want a perfectly smooth floor. We wanted a floor texture that would look more like leather after stain

Fig. 3.14: *The top two images show different approaches to using the slates as they were used on the roof ... both unsuccessful. Either the rough edge is exposed·as a hazard to walking barefoot or there is a flimsy cement coating over the dangerous edge area. In the lower drawing, the slate is set nicely into the concrete with gentle taps from a rubber mallet, and the concrete can be safely pointed right up to the slate's edges with a pointing knife. The long-protected underside of the slate is usually much more attractive than the top side.*

was applied. Hand troweling approximates the texture we were after much better than would a power trowel.

Finishing the Floor

First, using two flat plasterer's trowels, we hand-troweled almost the entire floor. Our intern, Nick Brown, was extremely good at this, and his wide wingspan, a function of his 6-foot 9-inch height, enabled him to reach far in towards the center of the building.

Next, we stretched nylon strings across the slab, as seen in Figure 3.15 and Figure 3.16. Two parallel strings, 11 inches apart, were stretched tightly to

Fig. 3.15: *Each spoke is made up of seven slates. The first one is shaped with the slate cutter to match the inner surfaces of the future walls, allowing an inch for pointing between the slate and the walls.*

nails on the forming boards marking the slate "spoke" locations along the four diagonals of the octagon. The extra inch of width gave us room to set the 10-inch-wide slates without upsetting the tight guide strings.

I used a pattern stick made of a 10-foot two-by-two to figure out and space the slates so that the innermost slates would all be the same distance from the center. There is a two-inch spacing between slates. The last slate of each spoke was also shaped to a dull point, giving a pleasing eight-sided star pattern around the future center post.

Once positioned, the slates were set into the concrete with gentle taps from a rubber hammer, which you can see in Figure 3.17. In that picture,

Fig. 3.16: *Jaki (left) sets the first slate of one of the spokes while Nick (right) measures for setting a slate on another spoke.*

Fig. 3.17: *Jaki points while Nick trowels.*

Jaki is pointing around the slates with a cordwood pointing knife (discussed in Chapter 6) while Nick trowels the wide open spaces near the center. Both workers are kept off the still-fresh concrete by cat-walking on doubled 2-by-8 boards supported by pieces of 2-inch Styrofoam®. The almost-finished floor is seen in Figure 3.18.

You readers may find it curious that we did not install any anchor bolts in the slab to assist in fastening the post-and-beam frame. There are two reasons for this: (1) The anchor bolts get in the way of troweling, making for rough or irregular concrete right in the very place where you want it flat and smooth. (2) Mr. Murphy, again, will do his devious best to make sure that

you put them in the wrong place. While unlikely in the case of the eight posts at the points, this is a very real possibility in the case of the door and window jambs. There is a better way, as you will see in the next chapter.

The footing forms can be safely removed on the second day after the pour. Staining the concrete and sealing the slates are discussed in Chapter 8.

Fig. 3.18: The slab is poured and troweled. Jaki points around the last couple of slates.

Timber Framing and Planking

Four Kinds of Posts

Timber posts that are square, rectangular or round in cross-section will not work well with a cordwood masonry octagon, as we saw in Chapter 1. Each of the "Four Methods" described in that chapter make use of an internal 45-degree angle, so that the cordwood masonry will bear directly onto the hidden sides of the posts.

Method One and Two posts (Figures 1.7 and 1.8) can be cut at a sawmill, as were ours, or they can be made at home by ripping off edge slabs of logs with one of the various chainsaw milling attachments available today. First, mark the small end of your log with the desired cross-sectional shape, incorporating the required 45-degree angle. Next, screw your 2-by-4 (or 2-by-6) guide to the log in such a way that the chain will rip the edge of one of the lines you have drawn. Try it by just tickling the end of the log with the cutting chain. If the cut is a little off, refasten your two-by guide just a little. Figure 4.1 shows me using my $29.95 "Beam Machine" to make such a cut for a Method One post, my favorite. (Beam Machine by Ted Mather, Box 16, Quathiaski Cove, BC V0P 1N0, Canada.)

Ted recommends an ordinary chain, not a ripping chain, to get a smoother cut. With a sharp chain on my Stihl 029 saw, I can make an eight-foot cut in about three minutes, so there is just six minutes of cutting to make a Method One post, plus a little time in marking it out and screwing

Fig. 4.1: *Using the "Beam Machine" to make a Method One post.*

the 2-by-4 guide in the right place. A couple of more cuts are required for Method Two posts, and setting up the 2-by-4 guide could be tricky. For these reasons — and for appearance — I prefer the Method One kind.

The workshop. All of our Method One and Method Two posts were made at the sawmill prior to our three-day "Timber Framing For the Rest of Us" workshop at Earthwood. The students and I made all of the Method Three and Four posts at the workshop. Morning sessions were in the classroom, and afternoon sessions were practical hands-on sessions. In three afternoons, we cut, raised and plumbed the eight posts; installed the eight girts; put in the ten vertical door and window jambs; installed the central post and capital;

and installed all 16 radial rafters. In other words, we completed the timber framing. Most of the 14 students were inexperienced, but all had a good aptitude to learn.

Method Three posts (Figure 1.9) are not difficult to make if you have small straight cylindrical logs or trees, and if you use good screws and a good electric drill. We did the work on the first afternoon of the Timber Framing workshop. (Figures 4.2 and 4.3) A student simply screwed a nominal two-by-four (actually 1½ by 3½ inches) to the side of a nice straight round barked cedar log having a somewhat consistent seven-inch diameter. I use self-countersinking three-inch screws from GRK Fasteners (1499 Rosslyn Road, Thunder Bay,

Fig. 4.2: A student screws a finished two-by-four to a seven-inch log.

Fig. 4.3: *A three-inch dowel is fastened to the post, using six-inch self-countersinking GRK screws.*

Ontario P7E 6W1, Canada. Website: grkfasteners.com; Telephone: 1-800-263-0463.) Five or six screws are plenty for our posts, which are all just 6 feet 6 inches in length.

Next, we screwed a three-inch cedar dowel to the two-by-four, using some six-inch GRK screws. The intermediary two-by-four acts as a spacer and helps the geometry to work out correctly. Our pieces came from a friend who has a company that makes cedar log homes, rails and other details requiring large dowels. Peeler cores from a plywood plant also make excellent dowels for this purpose.

Method Four posts make use of standard full-dimensional lumber. We use rough-cut material for the rustic look and to give a full eight-inch thickness to the post. Each post is made from a two-by-eight, two-by-six, two-by-four and two-by-two, as per the drawing, Figure 1.10. The best photo I have of one of these posts is Figure 4.4, and you will see another view at Figure 4.29 when we speak of rafter installation. Also, Figure 6.20 in Chapter 6 shows how a Method Four post looks from the exterior. Many people might think it is an eight-by-eight, but, as we discussed in Chapter 1, an eight-by-eight won't work well as an octagon post.

Fig. 4.4: *The Method Four post.*

To make two such posts, I bought five 8-foot rough-cut two-by-eights from sawyer Norm Davis. Two of them I left as two-by-eights. Two of them I ripped into a two-by-six and a two-by-two, using my circular saw. The remaining one I simply ripped down the middle, yielding two two-by-fours. If you want to make eight such posts, instead of just two, multiply all of the above piece numbers by four. You can make eight such posts from twenty 8-foot two-by-eights. Use nails or screws — I prefer screws — to fasten the members together. You need about five fasteners for each joint.

We made all of our posts from eight-foot-long material, as seven-footers are not a common item. (Remember that they wind up just 6 feet 6 inches tall.) Then we squared one end and tested it by actually standing it up. The cut should be good enough that the post stands on its own. If not, re-mark and re-cut that end and try again. Practice your technique on the first end, taking a couple inches off each time. When you've got a good end, measure 6 feet 6 inches from several places along the post, mark the opposite end, and connect the marks with a pencil and straightedge. *Carefully make your cut.* You only get one shot at the second end!

We'll describe fastening the posts to the slab in a moment, but before doing that, the empty slab serves as a great pattern for laying out the girts.

Laying Out and Cutting the Girts

The plate beams that connect the tops of the posts are more properly called *girts*. Two of them will always join over the tops of the posts and so must have a 112.5-degree angle cut into each end (or 67.5-degrees if using your protractor from the other side of the timber. Please see Figure 4.5 for clarification.)

As discussed in Chapter 1, the Stoneview plan calls for each of the eight walls to have an outer length of 8 feet 3 inches. Obviously, we must cut the trapezoidal-shaped girder (as see from above) from a timber of at least 8 feet 3 inches, and it is better and easier to start with a blank at least an inch or two longer.

First, I examined all four sides of each girder piece, and decided which sides I wanted to see inside and outside. The tops and bottoms of the girder would be almost entirely hidden, the exceptions being where girders also serve as door or window lintels.

To lay out my girders, I made pencil marks 8 feet 3 inches apart on the top of the exterior face. Then, with an angle square set at 67.5 degrees — check out Figure 4.5 again — I marked the ends of the girts, as seen from the top. Then, using a framing square, I dropped perpendicular lines onto the inner and outer surfaces of the girts, to guide my saw.

There are beam-cutting saws which will go through eight-inch material, but they are extremely expensive. You might be able to hire one at a tool rental store and make all your cuts in a few hours. I use a chainsaw with a bar at least sixteen inches long. Or, better, I use a chainsaw married to a cutting bench as seen in Figure 4.6. Using shims, the saw can be made to come through any square timber at a very precise right angle.

Fig. 4.5: "Octagon" girts are cut at an angle. The obtuse angle is 112.5 degrees (a right angle plus 22.5 degrees) while the acute angle, the one you get from a viewpoint from the opposite side, is 67.5 degrees (a right angle less 22.5 degrees.) When two such girts are butted against each other, a 45-degree bend is created on the outside of the girt system. By similar logical geometry, the internal angle where two girts meet is 135 degrees.

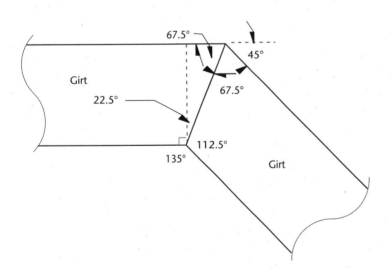

Once all eight girts have been cut to size and shape, they can be laid out on the octagonal slab prior to the posts being erected. We placed an 8-by-8 scrap of beam at the eight octagon corner locations, so that we could mock up the girt system at a comfortable, safe and sturdy working height. You can see a couple of girts set up in Figure 4.7.

All eight girts are set up in this way, completing the octagon. Care is taken that the points of this mock-up of the octagonal girt system are all in the same relationship to the eight points of the concrete slab. Because the perimeter of the slab is slightly larger than the perimeter of the timber frame, the points of the octagon girt system will be closer to the building's center by an inch or even 1½ inches. Keep this distance consistent all around.

Fig. 4.6: *The author makes a 67.5-degree cut through an 8-by-8 girder, using Bruce Kilgore's cordwood cutoff saw table. Students hold the timber steady on the table, assisted by another platform erected nearby. The angle of the timber in relationship to the table's length is 22.5 degrees. The author works to a pencil mark on the top of the beam.*

TOM HARRIS

Fig. 4.7: *Scrap 8-by-8 blocks are set up around the slab, at the octagon points. All of the girts can now be cut and fitted at this safe and convenient working level.*

Now, you may find, as we did, that the girts do not always butt up perfectly to each other. The angles, vertically or laterally, may not line up exactly right. You may see daylight between them. This is where an old chainsaw trick comes in handy, seen in Figure 4.8. With students lending their weight to the girts so that they don't move, I passed the chainsaw bar and chain through the imperfect joint. After doing all the imperfect joints in this manner, we tightened them up against each other once again. Now, the fits are much better. It might be necessary to pass the chains through some joints more than once before you have an acceptable join. For this reason, it is a good idea to cut the original 8 foot 3 inches outside measure a little on the long side, maybe a quarter-inch to a half-inch.

TOM HARRIS

Now, we number the girts according to their position in the octagon (N, NE, E, etc.) and set them aside while we install the eight posts.

Installing the Eight Perimeter Posts

Posts are kept from moving on the foundation by the use of vertical pins placed at the right locations. Some people install anchor bolts into the slab on the day that it is poured, but I don't do this, for two reasons: (1) Murphy's law dictates that they are sometimes put in the wrong location, especially with the more critical door frames and (2) It is hard to trowel smoothly in the important corner post locations with this pin in the way. Therefore, I install my pins by using lead expansion shields and lag screws sunk into sockets

Fig. 4.8: With students lending their weight to the process, the author passes his chainsaw between the two girts. Usually, one such pass will yield an excellent fit when the girts are drawn in together.

Fig. 4.9: *The author traces the base of a Method One post onto a piece of 240-pound asphalt shingle. Next, the damp-proof piece is cut out of the shingle with a razor knife (not shown).*

drilled in the cured concrete. Further, when posts are placed on a concrete slab, it is necessary (and a code requirement) to install what we call a "damp-proof" course between the post and the slab. I make my damp-proof material from pieces of leftover 240-pound asphalt shingle or roll roofing. I place the posts on a scrap of asphalt shingle and mark around it with a pencil. Then I remove the post and, with a razor knife, cut the damp-proof piece out of the shingle or membrane.

The following sequence accurately illustrates the post installation, although the pictures were taken in our garage after Stoneview was built because I failed to shoot the actual event. Heavy black lines represent the edge of the slab and post location.

Fig. 4.10: *A hole is drilled into the concrete with a masonry bit (not shown) and a leaded expansion shield is hammered flush with the concrete surface. A lag screw compatible with the expansion shield is turned into the shield with a wrench or socket set.*

Fig. 4.11: *After the head of the lag screw has been cut off with a hacksaw or grinder (not shown), the damp-proof course is pressed over the pin and into place on its footprint.*

Fig. 4.12: *Using concrete blocks to aid in positioning the post correctly over the corner, one person holds the post in place …*

Fig. 4.13: *… while another hits the top of the post with a heavy hammer, making an impression of the pin on the post's underside.*

Installing the Girts

With all eight posts standing vertically, we set the numbered girts into place, one at a time, duplicating what we had previously done down near ground level. Sometimes this meant a little adjustment to the plumb of the post, but, generally speaking, we had a good replication of our girt system where it belonged. Working off of a stepladder (scaffold), we put in two 12-inch GRK screws on each side of the butt joint between girts. So there are four such screws set into each of the eight posts, 32 screws in all.

Fig. 4.14: *Back to the actual Stoneview project! Next, a hole is drilled into the underside of the post at the impression made in the previous step. The post is reinstalled on the pin and held plumb while strong but temporary wooden diagonal braces are installed to hold it plumb and in place. The bottom end of the wooden brace is screwed to a stout 2-by-4 stake driven firmly into the ground. The top end of the bracing is screwed into the side of the post when the person looking at the plumb bubble calls the post plumb.*

Fig. 4.15: *The workshop team manhandles the final girt into place.*

Major Cut List for Stoneview:
Timbers for girts, rafters, window and doorframes and capital:

Girts:

8 x 8 white pine, planed four sides: 8 @ 8'5" (cut to 8'3" on site for use)

Rafters:

4 x 8 white pine, planed four sides: 8 @ 12'6"

4 x 8 white pine, planed four sides: 8 @ 12'0"

Door jambs and large window framing:

4 x 8 white pine, planed four sides: 8 @ 7'0" (can be made from 4 @ 8 x 8 x 14', ripped down the middle, then cut in half)

Extra 4 x 8 for the capital: 4 x 8 white pine, planed four sides: 2 @ 12'0"

Small window frames:

2 x 8 white cedar or pine, planed four sides: 4 @ 10'0" (will vary according to owner's window schedule)

Post material:

Method One and Method Two Posts:

Four large (12" small end) pine or cedar logs, custom cut as per text, 8'0" long.

Method Three Posts:

Two @ 7" diameter round

Two @ 3" diameter round

Two finished 2 x 4 studs as spacers

Method Four Posts:

Note 1: Finished perimeter post heights to be 6' 6", so 7-footers advised for squaring ends

Note 2: Assumes two each of the Four Post Methods. Adjust accordingly if a different post schedule is desired.

2 x 8 white pine, rough-cut: 5 @ 7'0"

    (Rip three of these, in the field, into 2 @ 2 x 2, 2 @ 2 x 4 and 2 @ 2 x 6)

Round center post (straight log or tree trunk):

Needs to be at least 7' high, so look for an 8-footer for trimming.

Roof deck:

2 x 6 v-jointed T&G spruce: 112 @ 10'0"

I have become very enamored with the quality of GRK fasteners. Their special thread allows them to be drawn easily with a ½-hp electric drill through an 8-by-8 girder and into the tops of posts. The star drive bits are non-slip and not prone to damage and the steel used with these screws has a high shear strength. At about $1.75 each, they cannot be called cheap, but to fasten all the girts to the posts for $56 can certainly be called a bargain, when time is factored in. With no pre-drilling required, it only takes 12 to 14 seconds to set a 12-inch GRK in place, maybe 20 minutes of actual drilling in all, including moving the ladder. Several of the students had a go at the screwing and all were impressed with the ease with which they went in.

Fig. 4.16: *A workshop student joins two girts over a post, using 12-inch GRK screws.*

An alternative to GRK fasteners is the TimberLok™ line of screws. (FastenMaster. 153 Bowles Road, Agawam, MA 01001; Website: fastenmaster. com) They are also a good screw, are less expensive and have a different hex head bit (supplied) to install them. While not quite as strong as the GRKs on shear, they are a good quality fastener. Our garage at Earthwood is built with them.

After the girts are all installed with the GRK screws, it is necessary to keep them from spreading by the use of truss plates joining two adjacent girts on their top side. We used 4- by 6-inch galvanized truss plates (sometimes called mending plates) with some 50-odd little holes for installing nails, as per Figure 4.17. The plate is quickly installed with a hammer, half of the plate on each side of the joint. Another style of plate, easier to use, has lots of little spikes sticking out of the underside. The installer simply whacks them in to the wooden members, half on each side of the join. An example of this can be seen in Fig. 5.12 in the next chapter.

Finally, bracing is needed to stop the building from "racking." The posts are already braced with long diagonal bracing to stakes driven in outside the building. To stop the posts and girts from moving around the perimeter, we installed smaller diagonal bracing, from post to girt, made from scrap one-by boards, which can be seen if you go back and look at Figure 4.4 or jump ahead to Figures 4.29 and 4.32.

Window and Door Framing

The Stoneview plan has four large windows and a three-foot wide door, all of which are centered in their respective panels. Each of these five components is framed by 4-by-8 vertical jambs, from slab to girt. All ten vertical four-by-eights are pinned to the slab as described above for the eight posts and all have damp-proof pieces between their undersides and the slab. In the singular case

Fig. 4.17: *A truss plate is used to stop two girts from spreading.*

of the door jambs, we used two pins for each jamb, to assure that their bases could not rotate, which would be a potential problem with getting the door to fit well.

The actual door and windows we used at Stoneview are described in more detail in Chapter 7, but, for framing purposes, it is important to note that the height to the underside of our girts was based on the 34½- by 77½-inch (6-foot 5½-inch) door we procured. Our 6-foot 6-inch post height, therefore, was a function of the (almost) 6-foot 6-inch high door. Most "six-eight" doors are actually 6 feet 7½ inches in height. With pre-hung units, the "rough opening" is actually 6 feet 10 inches (82 inches) and this would be the height of your posts. Our posts are four inches less than this, just 6 feet 6 inches, because we made use of a recycled door and trimmed it out ourselves within the door frame (girt and jambs). Make sure of the actual rough opening of your door by measuring the unit, adding one-half inch to the total actual height of the pre-hung unit. Never trust anyone's printed numbers. Murphy does printer's errors, too.

The large windows we procured filled most of the vertical space under the girt, so we made our 4-by-8 window jambs the same height as the door jambs: 6 feet 6 inches. Much later, during window installation, we kept the windows right up to the girts, by setting them on a 2-by-8 sill a few inches off the floor. Cordwood masonry eventually filled that few inches.

As the eight sides of our slab were fairly flat and level, we made all the jambs, ten in number, the same 6-foot 6-inch height as the posts. After the girts were in place, we marked the underside of the girts with the location of the 4-by-8 jambs, keeping the windows (or door) centered in the panel. We measured each jamb individually, in case there was a little variation in the slab, and installed it over its damp-proof course. At the top, two 12-inch GRK screws held the jambs fast to the girt and prevented them from rotating. The window jambs were "jammed" tightly into place and not otherwise fastened down. Eventually the heavy load of the building — and the cordwood masonry — would hold them in place. However, we actually tried the window itself, as seen in Figure 4.18. When we knew it fit, we stored it away carefully for final installation after the cordwood was completed. I just wanted to make sure there would be no nasty surprises later on.

With the door jambs, though, it was much more important to keep the jambs from shifting on the foundation. After fitting the jambs as well as possible on their damp-proof course, and checking for square and rough

Fig. 4.18: *Students "try" the actual window in its space, framed by long 4-by-8 window jambs.*

Fig. 4.19: *In one case, a slightly smaller window, we fastened the window "buck" or frame, made of 2-by-8 material, right to the underside of the girt.*

opening size for the actual door, we fastened the jambs to the foundation by a variation on our post-fastening method. Listen:

Fastening jambs to the foundation. It is not possible to fit the jambs over a pin from above, because the installed girt is in the way, so we cut two six-inch-long pieces of angle iron, one for the outside of each door jamb. This angle iron can be bought at hardware stores, usually in four-foot lengths. It is full of circular and oblong holes, offering several fastening options. I mark the location of two of the holes on the foundation, and, at those locations, install two leaded expansion shields as described previously. Now, using hex-headed lag screws of the appropriate diameter, and just ¼-inch longer than the depth of the shield, I fasten these six-inch lengths of angle iron firmly to the foundation. Finally, I use two $5/16$-inch-by-2-inch hex-headed lag screws to fasten the angle iron to the 4-by-8 door jambs. Drill a ¼-inch hole with a wood bit and turn the lags in with a socket wrench. Now the door jambs cannot move or turn. Incidentally, I do not recommend the use of door jambs less than a full three inches thick for this kind of construction. I have seen people use two-by material, only to find the jambs bend in under the load of the plastic cordwood masonry. When you come to install the door — and it does not fit — well, it tends to spoil the rest of the day.

You could do all of the window jambs by the method described for the door jamb, but we decided that it was unnecessary. The 2-by-8 windowsill stops the jambs from moving towards each other under the cordwood load, and the heavy roof keeps the jambs from moving in and out. This worked for us, but very cautious types might like to replicate the angle-iron method for all of the girt-to-foundation window jambs. Just be sure to install the sill and check for square and rough opening size before doing the cordwood infilling. Diagonal bracing should be used to keep door and window frames square during construction.

The Post and Capital

Even with a "lightweight" living roof, described in the next chapter, a clear ceiling span of 18 feet or more isn't doable with reasonably sized timbers and, in my view, unaffordable by the use of commonly available materials. Therefore, Stoneview's roofing has a center post to cut the clear span in half. Mushwood, our summer cottage, makes use of a post of 26 inches in diameter, broad enough to bear the 16 floor joists. It weighs several hundred pounds, and is a beauty, with its varnished surface exposed in all three rooms downstairs. But the task can be accomplished with a much smaller post, in combination with a capital of sufficient size.

Sawyer Norm Davis provided a lovely cedar log for our center post. It wasn't much use to him as a saw log because it had five inches of ant-infested center rot along its entire length, so Norm was happy to trade it for a book. We actually cut two "special feature" hollow eight-inch log-ends off the big (15-inch diameter) end and used them on either side of the entry door, with bottle-ends in the cleaned-out rotten core. We cleaned out the rot on the post, as well, and eradicated the ants. I calculated — incorrectly! — the height of the post so that, with the capital added, I would have my favorite earth roof pitch of 1.5:12. Due to an error in my figuring, we wound up with a pitch of 1:12, still good, but not what Jaki and I had hoped for. Our post is actually 7 feet 0 inches (84 inches) high and has a capital of 10½ inches thickness, giving a total column height of 94½ inches. The height of the wall where the rafters actually bear is 86 inches, or 8½ inches lower. The clear span (inner edge of girt to outer edge of the capital) is 102 inches. So the pitch of the roof can be expressed as 8½-inches of rise over 102 inches of run, which is exactly one in twelve (1:12). This has worked well, but if you want the 1.5:12 pitch instead, the post needs to be 12¾ inches higher than the top of the girt. Our post should have been 4¼ inches longer.

The capital is made of criss-crossed pieces of leftover rafter material, three in each course as seen in Figure 4.20. We fastened one course to the previous course using six-inch GRK screws. Three courses were built up in all to give us the full capital thickness. If I had had enough material to do a fourth course, I would have. The extra 3½ inches of column height would have put us very close to the desired 1.5:12 pitch.

After three courses were fastened together, the square block was trimmed to a 22½-inch-diameter octagon, using a chainsaw. This is the short diameter of the octagon, made up from three adjacent 7½-inch-wide pieces. Figure 4.21 shows the completed capital resting on top of the center post, which had been cut to length and set at the center of the building on a damp-proof course. Two anchor pins prevent the post from rotating.

Next, we fastened the capital to the post with four 12-inch GRK screws, as per Figure 4.22. About 1½ inches of the threaded end grabbed the solid parts of the cedar post below. Once the sixteen radial rafters are installed, the roof load is symmetrical and consistent all around. The screws, then, act as positioning pins.

Fig. 4.20: *A workshop student fastens the second of three courses of four-by-eights to the first course. A third course was then added.*

Fig. 4.21: *The octagonal capital effectively broadens the 15-inch diameter post to 22½ inches.*

Cutting and Installing the Rafters

Our nominally 4-by-8 rafters are actually 3½ inches by 7½ inches because the rough-cut members were planed on all four sides at the sawmill for appearance and uniformity of dimension. This was our design choice. You could actually use rough-cut four-by-eights instead, which would be slightly stronger and less expensive. You could clean them up with a power sander. The depth of the rafter might vary by a quarter-inch or so. If they are under

eight inches, you can install cedar shingle shims to make up the shortfall. If they are a little over eight inches, you can remove a little wood on the underside of the rafter where it bears on the capital or the girt.

Eight of the rafters need to be 12 feet 6 inches long and it is sufficient for eight of them to be rough-cut at 12 feet. Generally, local sawmills cut their 12-footers a few inches long, so pick through them so that you have half of them at 12 feet 6 inches or close to it. The different rafter lengths are a function

Fig. 4.22: *The author fastens the capital to the post with 12-inch GRK screws.*

of the long (point-to-point) and short (side-to-side) diameters of an octagon. Eight rafters run from the center post and extend over the points, while the other eight follow the line from the center over the mid-point of the girts. See rafter plan, Figure 1.4.

Rafters are installed in opposite pairs, that is: the north rafter is installed first, then, immediately, the south rafter is installed. Or you can clockwise-number them from 1 to 16. So rafter No. 1 is installed, then rafter No. 9. Next, do the east and west rafters (Numbers 5 and 13.) Both identification systems are shown in Figure 4.23. These first four rafters all have right-angle cuts made in them with the cut-off saw as per Figure 4.24. Note that we bring the rafter in at a slight angle to the saw, the angle being equal to the 1:12 pitch of the roof. By making every cut in this way, the rafters butt very nicely up against one another as seen later in Figures 4.25 and 4.26.

The first pair of rafters butt against each other over the center of the capital. As I recall, we also set the next two rafters in place and checked everything over before fastening them. We made sure the post was plumb and that we had sufficient roof overhang. To maximize our materials, we used the 12-footers first, (the so-called "short" rafters that pass over the centerpoints of the girts). These rafters require a 20-inch overhang. Later the "long" rafters (the ones cut from 12-foot 6-inch blanks, and installed over the octagon points) will require a 22-inch overhang. With a pencil, we marked out the 3½-inch-wide footprint at the midpoint of all eight girts, the pencil marks on the top side. (Mark 1¾ inches to each side of the girt's centerpoint.) We positioned the first four rafters on the capital and on the girts, and installed a 3½-inch-wide cedar shingle (or two) to shim under the rafter, better distributing its load onto the girt. I don't like notching rafters, called *birdsmouthing*, as this (1) weakens the rafter, and (2) can so easily be botched up, spoiling the rafter. We fastened the rafters to the girts and to the capital, using 12-inch GRK screws.

Installation of the first four rafters firms everything up a great deal, so it is a good feeling to have them in place. The next four rafters, designated NE, SE, SW and NW (or Numbers 3, 7, 11 and 15) are slightly shorter and have a slightly different shape on the ends placed at the center. Figures 4.23 and

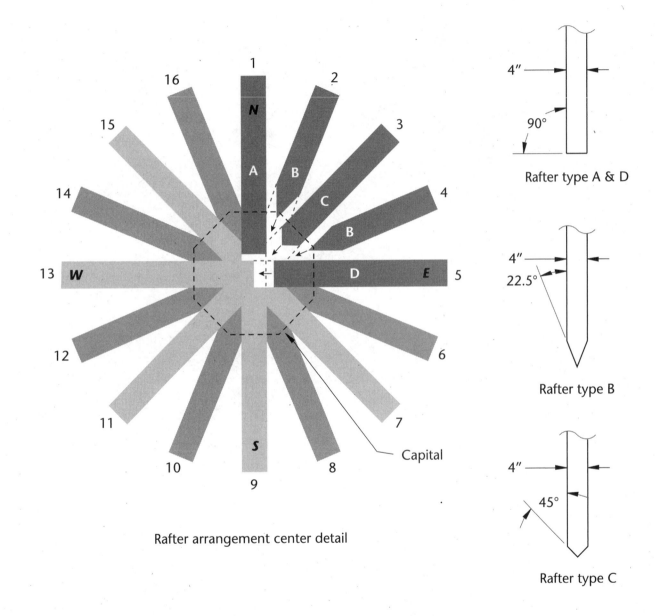

Rafter arrangement center detail

Rafter type A & D

Rafter type B

Rafter type C

Fig. 4.23

Fig. 4.24: *Students set the rafter on the cutting table at an angle equal to the 1:12 pitch — which is 4.8 degrees, by the way (although it is easier to lay it out in terms of pitch.) The cut remains square to the rafter's wide dimension.*

4.31 each show the shape of the inner cut, and the illustrations are fairly self-explanatory. The cuts can be made with a chainsaw, in a similar way to the cuts being made in Figure 4.28. Again, try to incorporate the 1:12 pitch into the cut so that the second set of four rafters butt nicely against the first four that you installed. When these four rafters are installed, the building really stiffens up, but there still remains all of the eight "long" rafters, and they have a slightly more difficult pointy cut to make.

The "long" rafters, the ones at the points, have their inner end sharpened to a wedge of 22½ degrees, as you can see in Figures 4.23 and 4.31. In Figure 4.28, I am making these angle cuts with a chainsaw.

Fig. 4.25: *Checking the position of the first four rafters.*

Fig. 4.26: *The first four rafters are screwed into the capital. A fifth rafter (the first of the next set of four) is tried for fit.*

These last eight rafters are passed up over the girt like all the others as per Figure 4.29 and wedged into the gaps between the first eight rafters. We actually tapped the ends of these rafters with a sledgehammer to tighten things up even more. Then both ends of each rafter are fastened down with a single 12-inch GRK screw. So, in all, it took just 32 screws to attach the 16 radial rafters. The rafters, now, define eight separate triangular planes for the installation of planking.

Note: In many parts of North America where strong winds are common, code may require more positive methods of tying posts to the foundation, girts to posts, and rafters to girts. Simpson Strong-Tie Co., Inc. (Telephone: 800-999-5099; Website: strongtie.com) and others provide metal fasteners for the purpose of meeting "continuous load path" regulations in wind-risk jurisdictions. Check with your local code enforcement officer. A more complete discussion of this subject, with examples and illustrations, appears in my book *Timber Framing for the Rest of Us* (New Society, 2004) at pages 75 through 84.

Fig. 4.27: *A student fastens a rafter down with a 12-inch GRK screw.*

Fig. 4.28: *The author stands above the rafter and makes a vertical cut, following lines that were marked on the top side of the rafter. The rafter is set up for cutting with the 1:12 pitch mocked up. This helps to incorporate that pitch into the compound cut, so that the pieces will fit together even more snugly over the capital.*

Fig. 4.29: *Students pass a rafter over the octagonal girt system.*

Fig. 4.30: *The 16 radial rafters meet over the capital.*

Fig. 4.31: *Top view of the rafters meeting over the capital.*

Fig. 4.32: *The completed post-and-beam frame, with rafters.*

Fig. 4.33: *Last day of the work-shop. The students are pleased with their accomplishments.*

Trimming and Shaping the Rafter Tails

The workshop was finished, but three or four of the students wanted to stay on and help install some planking on the following morning. There was just one remaining adjustment that needed to be made before planking could commence, and that was to trim all of the rafters (the rafter "tails") to their exact final length, so that each overhang was the same and so that the first plank of each facet would extend the same amount — one inch — over the edge of each rafter. I measured 22 inches out from the points of the girts and marked the underside of the rafter with a pencil. Next, I marked perpendicular lines upward on each side of the rafter to the top, finally connecting the lines on the rafter's top surface. This gave me a good guide for trimming the eight "long" rafters to their final correct length. Once those were done, I stretched a chalkline from the corner of one trimmed rafter to the corner of the next trimmed rafter. Someone snapped the line, showing the correct overhang for the intermediate rafters, the "short" ones.

I made all of my trim cuts with a chainsaw. Jaki wanted a bit of a flair to the rafter tails, for the sake of appearance, and I also made this cut with a chainsaw, seen in Figure 4.34. Finally, I cleaned up the cuts with my trusty Makita 4,500-rpm circular sander. Have I told you that this is one of my favorite tools? I use it constantly for trimming and cleaning wood, and for making good fits. See Figure 4.35.

NEAL PRESSLEY

Planking

I am very fond of 2-by-6 (actually 1½-by-5½-inch) tongue-and-groove (T&G) planking. It serves as an attractive visible ceiling over the exposed rafters, and as the roofing substrate for the application of the waterproofing membrane. The material is strong enough to carry the 115-psf living roof at the almost five-foot on center (5 feet 0 inches O.C.) planking span, which only happens on the overhang. We've used 2-by-6 T&G on Earthwood (and its sunroom addition), Mushwood, our office building and now, Stoneview. I purchased "seconds" from a sawmill at 40 percent off, but they really fit together well and are good looking. The few discolored pieces are hidden over the cordwood walls. Oh, and one other thing: on this particular building, it

Fig. 4.34: *A flair is cut into the rafter tail with a chainsaw.*

Fig. 4.35: *The author cleans up his chainsaw cuts with his trusty circular sander.*

works out really well to buy your planks in ten-foot lengths. Ten-footers work out perfectly with the dimensions, with practically no waste. The building's shape and dimensions are not conducive to the use of 4-by-8-foot sheets of plywood.

Installing the T&G planking on the first of the eight triangular roof facets is a little different from the second through seventh facets. And the eighth (final) facet is just a little different again.

First facet. We nail (or screw) the first long plank at the edge of the triangular facet, so that it overlaps all of the rafter tails by a full inch. This plank measures about 9 feet 9 inches in trimmed length, so the remaining students and

myself nailed down a ten-footer. In fact, we continued to nail down ten-footers as we worked our way up the facet, letting one end run on by the outer rafter of the facet more and more as we progressed up the gentle one-in-twelve (1:12) pitch slope. We went about halfway to the center with ten-footers in this way, as can be seen in Figure 4.36. Then we snapped a chalk-line from the center of the building to a point over the middle of one of the long rafters.

Next, I set the depth of my circular saw's blade so that it is just a tiny bit deeper — about $^{1}/_{16}$ inch — than the thickness of the planking, and we cut along the chalkline as seen in Figure 4.37. Figure 4.38 shows both edges

Fig. 4.36: *After fastening ten-foot T&G planks halfway up the facet, students snap a chalk-line from the center to a mark superimposed over the octagon corner points.*

Fig. 4.37: *Student Neil Pressley cuts off all of the "waste" pieces at once with a circular saw, giving a nice clean edge at the correct angle of 22.5 degrees.*

trimmed and the original "waste" pieces (not waste at all!) used to take us to the center. Next, chalklines would again be snapped along the planking above the middle of the rafter, the cuts made, and the triangular facet would be completed, all neat and tidy.

We screwed the first facet down, as we had plenty of nice 2½-inch countersunk GRK screws for the purpose, but, later, when my son Darin and I finished the project, we used 10-penny (3-inch) cement-coated nails. These nails grab very well into the 4-by-8 rafters, and by a full 1½ inches.

It is important to draw each T&G plank tight up against the previous course. A good way to do this (if they are giving you trouble) is by using a long — say ten-inch — log cabin spike as a "Class Three" lever. Set the plank in place up against the previous one. On the edge of the plank to be installed, drive the point of the spike into the 4-by-8 rafter — experience will teach you how far — until it grabs firmly. Get your nails started on the plank to be nailed. Then pull the top of the spike towards you with your left hand, drawing the new board tight in against its fellow. Still holding it tight, drive your nails. Repeat, as necessary, at the other rafter locations.

Another tip: never hit the wooden tongue with your hammer, which tends to mash up the wood. If you need to pound the tongue into the groove,

Fig. 4.38: The first facet is almost completed. It just remains to trim the ragged edges, as we did on the lower half of the facet.

use a foot-long piece of T&G scrap as an intermediary, and pound on that. Better, find out why the tongue is not going in easily. Usually the problem is further along the board and simply applying pressure down or up will ease it into place. This is a project most easily accomplished by two people working together.

The second through seventh facets ... are done in a manner similar to the first, except that one of each of the ten-foot planks needs to have that 22.5-degree angle cut put into one of its ends, so that it can be butted up to the 22.5-degree angle of the first facet. Thus, each facet is "turned" 45 degrees from the previous one. It is important to always make this cut the same way with respect to the placement of the tongue and the groove. I began with a grooved edge on the outside of my first board, and kept this pattern throughout the roof project. Again, fasten the plank down, with the untrimmed end running by the outer rafter of that facet. Use two fasteners at each location where a plank bears on a rafter. As with Facet No. 1, we trim the "waste" off when we get halfway up the facet. This waste, again, is used to complete the facet, similarly to the first facet.

The best way to get the 22.5-degree angle is with an angle square (also called a bevel square or angle finder), as will be seen in Figures 4.39 and 4.40 below.

The students left after the first facet and Darin and I completed the roof, a few hours each day, working our way around the building.

The eighth (final) facet ... is a little trickier, but, by now, you're experienced, so it's not so bad. There are two new twists:

The first twist is that it is necessary to begin the final facet at the center of the building with the shortest pieces and work your way out to the perimeter with ever-longer pieces. Consider: after the first seven facets are done, you could only get one long piece in on the outside. When you try to get the second-longest plank in, you can't. Topologically, it will not fit, no way, no how. The tongue gets in the way of placing a second plank. So, with great faith, we cut a small piece off the ten-foot board and use it first, saving the nine-foot waste for use later on.

Fig. 4.39: *After measuring the length of the short end of the next board, the author uses an angle square and pencil to mark it with the appropriate angle. This angle can always be taken off of the previously installed plank.*

Fig. 4.40: *Both ends of the plank are cut with a circular saw. Not shown: the plank is then fitted in tightly to the previously plank, and nailed down.*

Second twist: On the final facet, we need to measure the actual length of each piece to be fitted. Next, the angle cut needs to be marked and cut at each end. Then the piece is easily fitted — kind of wedged in, actually — between completed facets No.1 and No. 7. Figures 4.39 and 4.40, above, show how we did this on the final (sixteenth) facet of the 16-faceted floor at Earthwood.

This completes the post-and-girt and plank-and-rafter systems, a lot to cover in a chapter. You could put plastic or a tarp on the roof at this point, and begin the cordwood masonry (Chapter 6) under protection. At Stoneview, we installed all the layers of the living roof on quickly (except the earth), so that we had the protection without worrying about plastic or tarps blowing away.

5

The Living Roof

The Drip Edge

The living roof starts with something as mundane as a good drip edge. Now, while ten-foot sections of galvanized or baked-on enamel manufactured drip edge are available at a reasonable price, I prefer to make my own from eight-inch aluminum flashing. Two reasons: (1) Most manufactured drip edge is made for plywood, not 1½-inch-thick planking. It doesn't cover the edge well enough. And (2) the top surface of the common variety of drip edge is just three inches wide. That's a problem with the living roof, because the waterproofing membrane needs to be protected from the ultraviolet rays of the sun. By the time the nails are covered (by the membrane) on a three-inch-wide drip edge, the membrane is going to be very close to the edge of the roof and in danger of having sunlight beat upon it.

Eight-inch aluminum flashing is commonly available. I like it because I can bend two inches over the edge, extending the drip edge well past the 1½-inch-thick planking, and still have a full six inches on the roof. As you'll need around 82 feet, with overlap at the corners, you might as well buy two 50-foot rolls. I fasten the flashing with one-inch roofing nails driven about an inch from the top edge of the flashing (five inches in from the edge of the roof). Next, I bend the flashing over the sharp right-angled top edge of the planking, by applying firm pressure with my thumbs and forefingers. You can get a pretty good right angle on this flashing by using firm and even pressure.

Fig. 5.1: *The drip edge is in place, already covered by the membrane. The loose piece of flashing is a visual aid, showing how much of the flashing is covered. Circles show typical roofing nail locations; every nine inches is plenty.*

Later, the membrane covers the nails by two inches, leaving it a full three inches back from the edge of the building, as per Figure 5.1. Whether you use sods or retaining timbers to hold the roof on, the membrane will be well-protected from the damaging UV rays of the sun. Later, the overlapped edges can be tied together with two-inch-wide aluminum tape, as per Figure 5.2. Wonderful stuff.

The Waterproofing Membrane

I use and recommend the W.R. Grace Bituthene™ 4000 or 3000 waterproofing membranes. I have also used their less-thick Ice and Water Shield. All of these membranes consist of two layers of 2-mil black polyethylene laminated

over a sticky bitumastic material on the underside. A non-stick backing paper keeps the sticky surfaces from getting into trouble before you are ready to apply the membrane.

Fig. 5.2: *Aluminum tape (not duct tape!) joins adjacent pieces of drip edge made from aluminum flashing.*

The 4000 membrane is the best in terms of thickness and adhesion, and is also the most expensive. But each roll comes with a quart of acrylic "surface conditioner" with which the substrate is primed, the substrate being 2-by-6 tongue-and-groove planking in the case of Stoneview. With Bituthene™ 3000 and Ice and Water Shield, you really should prime the planking with something like the surface conditioner. If you can't find or order it easily, a bonding agent like Acryl-60® or DAP Bonding Agent will work.

We used Bituthene™ 4000 membrane, which is 3 feet wide and 65 feet long, about 195 square feet of material. However: one sheet of Bituthene™ must overlap the next by 2½ inches, cutting coverage down to about 180 square feet. Further, the ends of the individual trapezoidal pieces at Stoneview lap each other by six inches, so the useful area is decreased by another 7 percent or so, and we're down to 167 square feet of actual coverage from the roll. The true area of the roof is about 454 square feet. We need to divide by 167 square feet (effective coverage per roll) to get the number of rolls needed. 454 divided by 167 is 2.72 rolls. We were able to get away with two rolls because we scrounged enough leftover Ice and Water Shield from previous projects to finish the top. But the reader, starting from scratch, will need to procure three rolls, which will be plenty.

Installing the Membrane

The ideal time to apply any of the Bituthene™ membranes would be a cloudy day in the low 60s F. A small building like Stoneview is easily waterproofed in three to four hours with two people. The surface conditioner can be rolled on a couple of hours before the membrane is to be installed. Although dry, it may feel a little tacky, like the back of a sticky memo note.

Unroll the Bituthene™, with the backing paper still on, so that it is six inches longer than the point-to-point edge of the roof. The long (bottom)

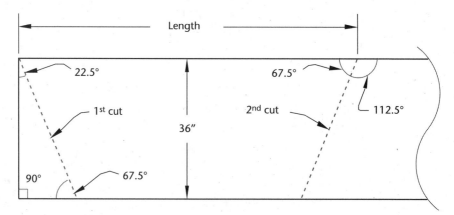

Fig. 5.3: *The first angle cut yields a small triangle of waste. Keep it for patching. Measure the total length of the first trapezoid, which should be about six inches longer than the point-to-point dimension at the drip edge. Use field measurements. Now, the next angle cut is already made.*

edge of the trapezoid should be just under ten feet, so your long edge should be around 10 feet 6 inches, but always go with actual field measurements.

Bituthene™ is neatly cut with a retractable razor-blade knife guided along a ruled four-foot straightedge. Both of these tools are among the most used tools in my kit, by the way, and essential for cutting waterproofing membrane. Cut over a piece of scrap board, such as a four-foot-long piece of one-by-six. There will need to be a 22.5-degree cut made at each end of this trapezoid. The first angle cut of the sheet yields a "wasted" piece, but keep it anyway, in case you need it for patches. The second cut is angled back to give a shorter top measure to the trapezoid. When you make this cut, you will have the next angle already cut and there will be no further waste until you get to the end of the roll. See Figure 5.3.

Start at the edge of the building, as you would, for example, with shingles. The first course of Bituthene™ is the toughest to install, as you are working close to the edge. On these first (relatively long) sheets, we roll it out with the backing paper still on and place it in its correct position on the roof deck, lapping the roofing nails of the drip edge by two inches. This will keep the membrane about three inches back from the edge. One person stands on the last two feet of the membrane, stopping it from moving or sliding. The other person rolls the membrane back up close to the standing person. Now, with the first person still standing, gently lift the 12 to 18 inches of the section of membrane that is still laying flat, and carefully peel back the backing paper and cut it away. Using many hands, keep the sticky part of the membrane from touching anything you don't want it to stick to, particularly itself. Carefully press the sticky part on to the primed roof deck and drip edge.

Next, the first person gets off the membrane and it is rolled back just a little further so that you can grab the backing paper where it has been cut. One person goes on hands and knees on the part stuck down. The other person begins to pull the backing paper off of the underside of the roll, as the kneeling person begins to press down the newly exposed sticky part while the membrane is unrolled for the second time. If you have not allowed the membrane to move during this process, it will follow its original alignment back and cover the nails just right. The person on knees presses the membrane down hard with the heels of his or her hands, working from the middle of the sheet towards the edges. When the sheet is fully laid, both people can go around the edges again with the heels of their hands. Try not to touch the caulked factory edges. They are very sticky, especially on hot sunny days.

Proceed with the other seven pieces that make up the first course, always lapping the previous sheet by six inches at the ends. This effectively means that you are lapping from one wooden triangular facet to the next by a three-inch lap over the long joint where planks meet. The next sheet laps three inches past that joint in the other direction, giving a six-inch lap where trapezoidal sheets of membrane meet end to end.

The second course can be applied in the same way, but you overlap the first course by 2½ inches. The top edge of each sheet has a white line to use

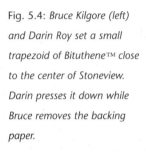

Fig. 5.4: *Bruce Kilgore (left) and Darin Roy set a small trapezoid of Bituthene™ close to the center of Stoneview. Darin presses it down while Bruce removes the backing paper.*

as a guide for the overlap. Continue doing the end laps as already described above. When the sheets get quite a bit shorter, further up the roof, you can cut the trapezoid to fit and then turn it over to remove the backing paper. Then turn it back over, sticky side down. Two people, each holding two corners with their hands, can now talk to each other and put the leading edge down to the 2½-inch lap line. One person needs to call the sheet for length, that is, the lap three inches onto the next roofing facet. Figure 5.4 shows the membrane going down at Stoneview.

After all the sheets are pressed down, all of the cut edges need to be caulked with Bituthene™ mastic, as seen in Figure 5.5. You'll need two or three 11-ounce tubes (or one large 32-ounce tube) for a project of this size.

Fig. 5.5: *The author caulks the cut edge of the Bituthene™ with the compatible mastic from W.R. Grace.*

Fig. 5.6: *Jaki and Darin feather the edge with our cordwood masonry pointing knives, approximating the factory edge of the Bituthene™ membrane. The mastic stops the edge from rising up.*

After a bead of caulking is laid down, we feather it into something looking like the factory edge, using a common non-serrated butter knife that has had its last inch of the blade bent to a 15-degree angle. This prevents the edge of the sheet from raising up or "fish-mouthing." See Figure 5.6.

The Bituthene™ needs to get covered as soon as possible to protect it from the sun. UV rays will deteriorate the surface, and hot direct sun can cause blistering quite quickly. We took care of this by getting the Styrofoam® insulation (see next section) on right away.

Top: *The buildings, raised bed garden, lawn, and stone circle are all reclaimed from the original gravel pit, five feet lower than the wooded area. The Stoneview site is just off-picture to the left.*

Bottom: *Stoneview with its living roof.*

Top left: *Dining area with decorative wall behind*

Top right: *The stained concrete floor is bright and cheerful.*

Bottom right: *The window with the greatest heat loss is fitted with a reflective insulated panel for wintertime use.*

Top far right: *We tell guests that these two dragons were born of the egg above them. In truth, they are naturally stained hardwood log-ends.*

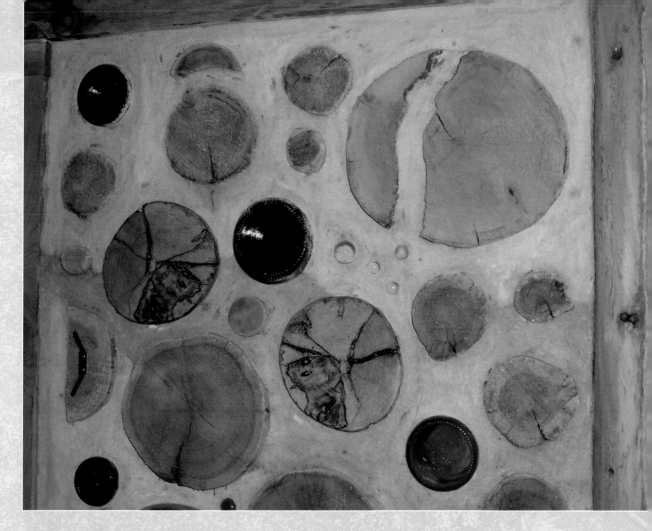

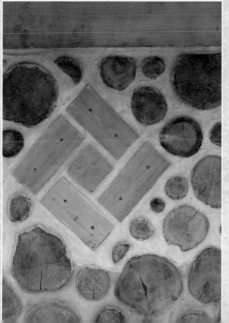

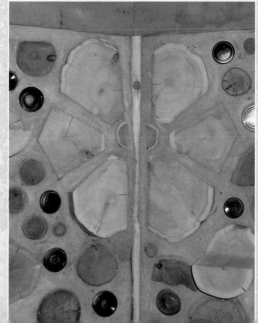

Bottom left: *This diamond pattern is pre-made on a bench and installed in one piece.*

Bottom Right: *This flower design is made of six log-ends left over from Method One and Method Two posts. Four of the log-ends were screwed to the post before the cordwood masonry commenced.*

Top: Jaki weeds
the bountiful crop
of wildflowers,
summer of 2005.

Bottom:
The sedum roof
at Stoneview,
summer 2007.

Fig. 5.7: *Any projection through a living roof is a potential leak and detailing (waterproofing and drainage) has to be done very carefully. As our Metalbestos chimney has an outside diameter of 8 inches, I cut a hole of 12 inches in diameter through the Bituthene™ and planking. I use a reciprocating saw, often called, generically, a sawzall, actually a brand name. The RSP (Roof Support Package) shown consists of a section of stovepipe with two adjustable ears or flanges, which can be screwed to the deck. The adjusting feature enables the stovepipe to be plumbed.*

If You Want a Chimney …

We wanted the option of heating Stoneview with a woodstove, making the guesthouse available for year-round use. We're glad we did. If you want to do the same, follow these steps (see figs. 5.7, 5.8, 5.9) for the installation of a Metalbestos chimney.

Fig. 5.8: *After the stovepipe is plumbed, the compatible Metalbestos flashing cone (the one for shallow-pitched roofs) is installed with roofing nails. Next, I cover the roofing nails, and flash the aluminum flashing cone to the membrane using 5-inch-wide strips of Bituthene™ membrane. Bituthene™ mastic all around the edges completes the waterproofing. The "storm collar" (part SC) sheds water away from the flashing cone, so it doesn't run down the stovepipe and into the building.*

Fig. 5.9: *We'll jump ahead just a bit to show how to provide good drainage around the stovepipe area. I made a 24-inch-square box around the stovepipe with pressure-treated 1-by-6 material and placed a couple of inches of #2 (1 inch) crushed stone over the drainage matting, discussed later. Water quickly travels in the drainage matting to the edge of the building.*

Insulation

We placed two inches (R-10) of Dow Styrofoam Blueboard® over the part of the roof where heat loss can occur from the room below, and one inch of the same foam right out to the edge of the building. While the overhang does not strictly need insulation, the foam works as a protection board for the membrane and also diminishes the amount of freeze-thaw cycling that can affect the membrane over the winter. Styrofoam® is an *extruded* polystyrene, but not the only one available. I do not recommend "beadboard," also called EPS or *expanded* polystyrene. It is more prone to saturation and loss of insulation value.

We scored a really good deal on one-inch-thick 2-by-8 sheets of Styrofoam® at a local supplier. One inch was appropriate for the overhang, anyway. The main part of the job would have gone faster with 4-by-8 sheets

of 2-inch-thick material, but we could not ignore the almost half-price buying opportunity.

First, we covered the entire roof, right to the edge, with an inch of the extruded polystyrene. We soon worked out a pattern of cutting the sheets to eliminate wastage, seen in Figure 5.10. The one-inch sheets are easily cut with a sharp new blade on your razor knife. (Two-inch sheets are more easily cut with any common general-purpose handsaw.)

Is it worth the extra cost of putting three or four inches of Styrofoam® (R-15 to R-20) on the roof? For a small building like Stoneview, I'd say it is not. As described, the roof insulation is about twice the value of the wall insulation, as it should be. The weak link for heating is probably the large windows we selected. But, as things are, the building is quickly and easily heated with the small woodstove.

Fig. 5.10: *Jaki joins the edges of the Styrofoam® pieces with good old-fashioned duct tape, holding them together until they are covered. Next, we put a second one-inch layer over the part of the roof without overhang, covering or overlapping the joins of the first course by a few inches.*

Fig. 5.11: *Several black polyethylene sheets, lapped by 18 inches, create the base of the drainage layer. Keep the shingle principle in mind.*

The Drainage Layer

The drainage layer begins with a sheet of inexpensive 6-mil black polyethylene, laid right on top of the Styrofoam®. We did it with several sheets, overlapping by 18 inches, as seen in Figure 5.11. Keep slope in mind in creating laps. Think like water would. This relatively inexpensive plastic is the base of the drainage layer. Water entering the drainage layer rides the poly quickly to the edge of the building, where it drips off of the edge.

The use of two inches of heavy crushed stone as a drainage layer (which we used successfully at the Earthwood house) adds an extra 20 pounds per square foot and defeats the intended purpose of a lightweight living roof at Stoneview. To reduce load, I use one of the composite drainage materials made by several companies. We selected Enkadrain® 3615R drainage matting from Colbond, Inc. (P.O. Box 1057, Enka, NC 28728; Telephone:

800-365-7391; Website: colbond-usa.com). This product consists of a 0.4-inch-thick mesh of tough recycled polypropylene covered by a filter fabric bonded to its top side. More recently, on a subsequent building, we used Enkadrain® 3811R, which has the fabric bonded to both sides. I like this feature, as it protects the 6-mil black poly better.

As with the membrane, eight trapezoidal pieces of Enkadrain® make up each complete octagonal course of the drainage layer, beginning at the bottom. Start it right at the edge of the roof. Even on the relatively shallow (1:12 pitch) roof, the small pieces of Enkadrain® tended to slide down towards the edge. We ended up splicing them together by overlapping the ends of the pieces by three or four inches over a 24-inch piece of one-by wooden scrap. I used short nails with large plastic washers to tack the pieces together over the scrap. Figure 5.12 shows this lap and two of the nails with large plastic washers.

Fig. 5.12: *Trapezoidal pieces of Enkadrain® composite drainage matting are tacked together using two nails with large plastic washers. The nails go into a 24-inch piece of one-by-two. Four-by-four pressure-treated retaining timbers are fastened to each other with small mending plates, also called "truss plates."*

Later, in a phone conversation, a Colbond representative suggested that I could have used double-sided tape to tack the Enkadrain® to the plastic. This is a good suggestion, but I think it would work better with the Enkadrain® 3811R drainage composite, which has a filtration mat on both sides. I can't imagine the rough tough polypropylene mesh sticking very well to the tape.

Retaining the Earth

Loose topsoil can be placed on the roof once the drainage layer is in place, but it will tend to fall off the roof at the edge if not retained in some way. I have used both retaining timbers and moss sods to retain the earth. Jaki and I like the moss sods, and we have a place to cut them in part of the old gravel pit we reclaimed to build Earthwood. However, it was late autumn, past growing season, and we wanted to get the earth on the roof for the winter so that it would hold the lightweight layers in place and be ready to plant first thing in the spring. The fastest, easiest and safest way to do this was by the use of pressure-treated retaining timbers. I selected eight straight ten-footers at the supply yard, and cut them to the right size and shape. On our roof, the long length averaged about 9 feet 10 inches, but you should measure and cut each one. Set your angle square for 22.5 degrees to get the short length. The eight retaining timbers are tied to each other with mending plates. The angle cut and the mending plate can be seen in Figure 5.12. The four-by-fours are tied to each other, creating an equally loaded tensile ring all around the roof, and are supported by the Enkadrain®, so that water can travel under them, but they are not fastened down through the roof layers to the planking.

We have also had good success on many living roofs by using moss or grass sods around the edge. They knit together and keep the loose topsoil from falling off. This approach is best taken in the spring, at the same time that the earth is installed.

Installing the Topsoil

Besides the use of a composite drainage matting, which weighs just ounces per square foot, the other key to a lightweight roof is using a minimal amount of soil. And the key to that is to plant drought-resistant plants, discussed below.

I bought a load of light sandy-loam topsoil from a local farm and had it dumped near the building. Then I made a stairway up to the roof, using a sturdy wood picnic table as a landing and wooden steps borrowed from our earth-roofed office building. I carried most of the earth up onto the roof by myself, using two 5-gallon plastic buckets. Friend Bruce Kilgore was a welcome help one afternoon. In all, it took about 450 bucket-loads of soil to cover the roof to a light fluffy 5½ inches depth. I positioned 24 six-by-six-by-eight blocks on the roof, right on the drainage matting, three equally spaced on each facet. These "depth gauges" actually measured 5½ inches in thickness, so I raked my soil even with their tops, or 5½ inches of soil in all. Later, I pulled the blocks — all except one — and filled the holes with more soil.

Fig. 5.13: *The author hauled about three-quarters of the soil onto the roof in 5-gallon buckets. Friend Bruce Kilgore did the rest.*

Fig. 5.14: *The author levels the light airy soil to the top of 24 "depth gauges," actually 5½ inches thick.*

At two bucket-loads per trip — for balance — it took 225 trips up the stairs. I spread the task over three days. See Figure 5.13 and Figure 5.14. We mulched the roof against erosion and left it for the winter.

By springtime, the rain and snow load had compacted the light fluffy soil to a uniform depth of 3½ inches, the same thickness as the eight pressure-treated retaining timbers. The depth gauge block that I had left behind showed clearly the amount of settling. It is interesting that the final compacted soil depth was 64 percent of its original depth as loose non-compacted topsoil. And thus it has remained.

The Lightweight Living Roof

Jaki planted chives, sedum and wildflowers (from a can of seeds) on the roof the following spring, in 2005. The wildflowers took over and were spectacular, but the other plants survived too. The next spring (2006), we weeded the roof and planted a lot of sedum. We selected sedum and chives for our roof, because these plants retain moisture in their succulent leaves, taking them through long rainless periods. We don't want to get into a watering situation on the roof.

Why not keep the wildflowers? In our experience over 25 years, they are wonderful the first year, so-so the second year, and very few wildflowers come back after that. Grasses take over the roof and there is no getting rid of them. Also, the grasses and wildflowers may not take you through a drought situation as well as the sedum. With our thicker "heavy" roofs (six to seven inches of soil), this has not been a problem. Eventually, if you don't mow, natural indigenous wildflowers come in on their own, in amongst the grass, but survival is kind of hit-and-miss with just 3½ inches of soil. Incidentally, in Europe, people are growing living roofs of sedum on as little as an inch of soil! Hard to believe, but true.

We got our sedum from Emory Knoll Farms, 3410 Ady Rd., Street, MD 21154. Ed Snodgrass is knowledgeable and a pleasure to work with. Call them at 410-452-5880 or go to greenroofplants.com. Ed sent us 450 plants, 5 different varieties of sedum. There are over 400 varieties of sedum. The garden ornamental called Hens and Chicks is a well-known example. Some sedums can get quite large and bushy. You want "ground cover sedum" and, in particular, varieties that are hardy in your growing zone. The 29 clumps of chives that we planted all came from a single large clump from our garden. They are doing very well on Stoneview's roof and some guests have picked the chives to make their eggs or sandwiches more tasty. Figures 5.15 and 5.16 show Jaki planting chives and sedum. Figure 5.17 shows several varieties of the sedum

Fig. 5.15: *Jaki plants chives on the Stoneview roof.*

Fig. 5.16: *A small sedum is planted.*

Fig. 5.17: *Fall of 2006. Five different varieties of sedum have spread over the roof. The picture was taken after a severe weeding and just as autumn leaves began to fall. See also the last page of the color section.*

and some chive plants, at the end of the first summer, after weeding. The leaves are beginning to fall on the roof. Incidentally, our five varieties are quite distinctive from each other. They flower with different colors, especially yellow, pink and an orangey-red.

We placed approximately 60 "stepping stones" on the roof, consisting of about 30 roofing slates and 30 one-inch slabs of the local red Potsdam sandstone. These stepping stones enable us to move about the roof without crushing the sedum, and they help maximize the value of a rainstorm, by shedding the water from their area to the adjacent plants. You can see some of the roofing slates in Figure 5.17.

The Stoneview roof is our favorite living roof of ten that we have at Earthwood, but that may be because we give it the most care. The other roofs are lovely, too, and require practically no maintenance. The sedum roof does require a lot of weeding for the first couple of years, but once the little plants grow together into a continuous ground cover, the weeding is very much less. You get a kind of patchwork mosaic of different kinds and colors of sedum. The chives seem to be compatible.

Fig. 5.18: *Jaki weeds the bountiful crop of wildflowers, summer of 2005.*

Fig. 5.19: *Close-up of sedum in amongst the wildflowers.*

Fig. 5.20: *Wildflowers abound on the Stoneview roof, summer of 2005.*

Cordwood Masonry

Chapter 5 covered the living roof installation from soup to nuts. In the actual event, we began to do some cordwood masonry as soon as the Bituthene™ membrane was safely protected from the sun's harmful UV rays. The point, repeated here for emphasis is: The post-and-beam frame allows the roof to go on before any cordwood is done. The cordwood masonry, therefore, is installed under the umbrella protection of the roof, a huge advantage.

Cordwood Masonry Overview

There are other "natural" and "green" wall systems that can be employed within the timber frame besides cordwood masonry: light clay, strawbale, cob and others. You can also fill the spaces in with a more conventional framing, wood siding, insulation, vapor barrier and sheetrock. But Stoneview wouldn't be Stoneview if it was not done in cordwood, and cordwood is the only external wall system that I feel I can speak to with some authority.

"For those who came in late," I'll repeat my time-worn definition: Cordwood masonry is that ancient building technique by which walls are constructed of short logs — called "log ends" — laid up transversely in the wall, much as a rank of cordwood is stacked. The wall gets its exceptional thermal characteristics from the insulated mortar matrix. Besides energy efficiency, cordwood walls are esthetically pleasing, easy to build, low in cost and environmentally sound.

One more definition is essential. A genuine cord of wood, sometimes called a *full cord*, is a stack four feet wide, four feet high and eight feet long. A *face cord* (sometimes called a *rank*, a *rack* or a *rick*) is four feet high by eight feet long by a stack width equal to the length you cut the logs: 8 inches, 12 inches, 16 inches, whatever. Knowing these terms is really important when you are buying firewood, and equally so when estimating cordwood for construction, as seen below.

There, with the boilerplate behind us, we can proceed to the practical side of the building method, as it applies to Stoneview.

The Cordwood

Because Stoneview is a relatively small guesthouse with just a 327 square foot footprint, we chose eight-inch-thick cordwood walls, worth about R-8 as insulation. (The wall thickness reduces actual usable interior area to 283 square feet.) This is in scale with the size of the building and the roughly R-15 roof insulation (Styrofoam®, planking, earth, plants, etc.). For those of you who think that's woefully inadequate for northern New York, I have three comments. (1) Our sauna has eight-inch cordwood walls and we can get it up to 190-degrees plus in two hours with our Nippa wood-fired sauna heater; (2) You could go with 12-inch walls if you prefer, but you would need to either knit the cordwood around the corner posts described in Chapter 4 or broaden the post system (and lose about seven percent, or 21 square feet, of useful area); and, (3) as built, we can use the building year-round, with just a small woodstove to heat it. Performance is discussed in Chapter 9.

So how much cordwood do we need? Framed as described — and with four fairly large windows, one small window and one three-foot door — I can report that the actual area of cordwood masonry at Stoneview is 244 square feet. We divide that number by 32 — there are 32 square feet on the side of any cord — yielding a preliminary estimate of 7.625 face cords. Now, because there are substantial mortar joints in the wall as well as log-ends, we can safely take 80 percent of the preliminary estimate, or 6.1 face cords. (7.625 x .80 = 6.1) In reality, six face cords would be plenty, with enough to discard log-ends that you are not happy with for one reason or another. Six face cords of eight-inch wood equals a full cord, which, you will remember, measures four feet by four feet by eight feet.

We used all white cedar (*arbor vitae*) for our cordwood. It is the best species we have found for the purpose as it has the highest R-value and is the most stable with respect to shrinkage and expansion. Although it does grow on our property, we got our cedar from a local log home company. Once or twice a year, I go down to their yard with my pickup truck and clean up "ends and pieces" of perfectly good dry, and usually fully barked cedar, just for taking it away. With eight-inch log-ends, you can get one or two useful log-ends out of almost any piece of scrap, but some of the "scrap" is over four feet long, yielding at least six log-ends. With cedar, there is no potential wood expansion problem with fully-seasoned wood — small pieces dried a year or more.

If white cedar is not available, choose from the lightest airiest woods that you have. Light airy woods are better as insulation and more stable than dense hardwoods. Be careful about the hardwood/softwood designation. Some "hardwoods" can be light and airy, such as quaking aspen, whereas some "softwoods," like southern yellow pine, can be quite dense and hard. Hard dense woods, usually characterized by narrow annual growth rings, are poor as insulation and tend to shrink — and expand — more than the airy species.

A more complete discussion of woods and drying times are discussed in *Cordwood Building: The State of the Art* (New Society, 2003). There is also a lot of good info — free! — in Q and A format, in my cordwood masonry column on greenhomebuilding.com.

It is easiest to bark (or *debark*, same thing) the wood in longer pieces, then cut it into the short 8-inch log-ends. Logs are easiest to bark in the spring, when the sap is rising, and most difficult in the autumn. My favorite tool for barking is my pointed mason's trowel. Get the point under the bark and you can pull wholesale strips off of an eight-foot log. In favorable conditions, the log can be barked in two minutes. At unfavorable times of the year, try soaking the logs (fully immersed) for a week. This usually facilitates the process considerably.

At Stoneview, the log-ends are almost all rounds, with diameters varying from an inch up to 22 inches. Most are in the three- to nine-inch-diameter range. You can use split wood instead of rounds, or you can mix splits and rounds. Just try to keep the pattern and texture the same throughout the building. (An exception to this rule would be to do each of the eight panels with a different texture or style: rounds in this one, splits in the next, etc. It's okay if it looks like you meant it.)

We cut the wood into eight-inch log-ends with a chainsaw. We borrowed Bruce Kilgore's cordwood cut-off saw, seen in Figure 4.6. His chainsaw is mounted to a bench by way of "pillow blocks" as a pivot mechanism. Each cut is dead straight and an adjustable stop can be fastened to the end of the bench, so that every log-end is exactly eight inches long, a real advantage. Detailed instructions of how to make this cut-off saw appear at pages 74 to 77 of *Cordwood Building*. Alternatively, you can mark the long log every eight inches with a marker or crayon, have someone hold it on a saw bench, and then destroy each mark as you cut through the log. The chainsaw removes about a quarter inch of wood — the *kerf* — so you will end up with pieces about 7¾ inches long, which is okay. (If you want true eight-inchers, add an extra ¼-inch to each measure.)

Stack and dry the cordwood in single ranks, with the top of the pile covered, but not the sides. Let the sun and wind get to the wood. As eight-inch-wide ranks are unstable, it is good to stack two ranks on a row of pallets and tie the ranks together with frequent "stickers." Stickers are small diameter sticks cut to a convenient length — say 32 inches — which act as stabilizers, tying one rank to the next, and lending strength to both. Be sure to leave at least 16 inches of space between ranks, for proper aeration.

The final act of preparation, most easily done after the wood is dry, is to clean the little "hairs" off the end of the log with a rasping tool like a Stanley Sure-Form® Scraper, as per Figure 6.1. These little hairs, caused by the chainsaw, get in the way of pointing and make the wall look untidy.

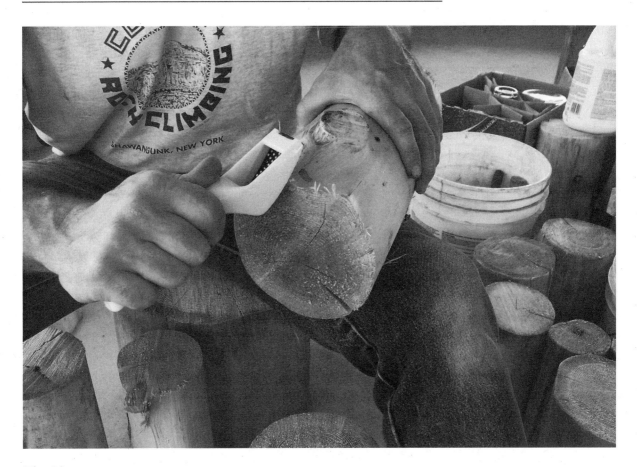

The Mortar

At Stoneview, we predominantly used our standard Portland cordwood mortar. The recipe — equal parts by volume — is 9 sand, 3 soaked sawdust, 3 builder's lime, 2 Portland cement. Let's discuss these ingredients in more detail.

Sand. Use fine sugary sand which yields a more "plastic" mortar, as opposed to coarse grainy sand, which tends to produce a crumbly mortar, is harder to work with and is more wasteful. Masonry sand is perfect. Also, light-colored sand will yield a lighter color mortar, an advantage because cordwood masonry, like stonework, tends to be a "light-sucker."

Fig. 6.1: *Holding the rasping surface of the scraper at a 45-degree angle to the log-end, cut the little quarter-inch "hairs" off the edge of the log with a firm pulling motion.*

Sawdust. The sawdust used as a mortar additive needs to be from one of the "lighter and airier" woods that we described above as being better for log-ends. The purpose of the sawdust is to slow — or *retard* — the set of the mortar. Slowing the cure reduces mortar shrinkage, and, therefore, mortar cracking. We have not had good luck with hardwood sawdust as a mortar-retarding agent. In fact, the hardwood sawdust —the kind from a circular sawmill, anyway — just makes the mortar grainy to work with.

Pass the sawdust through a half-inch screen and totally immerse it, at least overnight, in an open-topped leak-proof container such as an old bathtub or a 55-gallon drum. Complete each day's work by preparing enough soaked sawdust for the next day's work. It is okay for the sawdust to stay soaked for a month or more. If it starts to blacken or smell bad, rinse it and use it. Or replace it. If you do not have favorable sawdust for the purpose, use a com-mercial cement retarder or the lime putty mortar, both described below. If in doubt, try a test batch, with cordwood. If shrinkage cracks are going to occur, you will know it within five to seven days. Mortar cracks aren't the end of the world, but they can be eliminated if you use the right mortar mix.

Lime. It is imperative to use builder's lime, also called mason's lime and, particularly, Type S lime. You get it where cement is sold, not from an agri-cultural supplier. Agricultural lime will not calcify in the same way as mason's lime; your mortar will be very much weaker.

Portland. You can be sure of the strength quality of Type I or Type I/II Portland cement. A one-cubic-foot bag always weighs 94 pounds. If it weighs 70 pounds, or 80 pounds, you probably have some type of masonry cement. Masonry cements vary in strength according to their type, and the recipe would be slightly different: 3 masonry cement and 2 lime instead of 2 Portland and 3 lime. We strongly recommend the use of Portland cement, because you can be sure of what you've got. Do not let anyone sell you "mor-tar mix," which is a mixture of sand and masonry cement.

We have been mixing all our mortar in a wheelbarrow for over 30 years. We do this because we have better quality control, and we have a more pleas-ant building site. Plus, we don't have to worry about the "infernal frustration engine" breaking down. And, in any case, you need a wheelbarrow to get the mortar to the wall. When working alone, it is handy to work right out of the barrow.

Dry lime and Portland are both nasty materials to ingest. Don't throw them into the wheelbarrow, as they create a toxic dust cloud. It's a good idea to wear a dust mask during mixing. And always wear cloth-lined rubber gloves throughout the mixing (and laying) process, because Portland, lime and mixed mortar are all heavily alkaline and can burn your skin. You can get nasty little "cement holes," which are painful and take days to get better.

We use long-handled garden spades for measuring out the ingredients, being careful to use equal-sized rounded shovelfuls. We use a "wet" spade for the sawdust, and an equal-sized "dry" spade for the other goods. (If your sand is quite wet, you may want to use the wet spade for both sand and sawdust.) We introduce the ingredients into the barrow in the following cadence, equal parts by volume:

- 3 sand, 1 soaked sawdust, 1 lime, 1 Portland
- 3 sand, 1 soaked sawdust, 1 lime, 1 Portland
- 3 sand, 1 soaked sawdust, 1 lime

By using this cadence, the batch is a long ways towards being dry-mixed as soon as the ingredients are introduced into the barrow. Now, with an ordinary garden hoe, mix the ingredients. Turn them over with the hoe, drawing them from one end of the wheelbarrow to the other. (The expensive mason's hoes, with the two big holes in the blade, are meant for brick and block mortar; a regular garden hoe is better for cordwood mortar, and much cheaper.) When this "dry mix" has a consistent color throughout — it only takes a minute or two — it's time to add water.

In the center of the dry mix, make a little crater with the hoe. Add a good splash of water, maybe a gallon, and, again, chop everything back and forth with your hoe. The amount of water to use depends on how wet your sawdust and sand are. With dry sand, you will need quite a bit, with wet sand, very little. I have seen sand so wet that we didn't need to add any water. In that case, it's best to drain most of the sawdust water out of the spade before adding it to the mix; otherwise, it may be difficult to dry the batch sufficiently for use. It is a good idea to keep your sand pile covered with a water-shedding tarp.

We are looking for a fairly stiff — yet plastic — "stone mortar," not a wet "brick" or "block" mortar. When you think it's right, perform the "snowball test." Toss a snowball-sized sphere of mortar three feet up into the air — one meter in Canada! — and catch it in your gloved hand. If it crumbles when you catch it, it is too dry, and you will need to add water. If it goes "Sploot!" in your hand, like a fresh cow pie, it is too wet. In this case, you will have to add more dry goods (no wet sawdust) to stiffen it up, in the same proportion as the original mix. (Hint: Use the driest sand off the top of the pile, to stiffen soupy mortar.) If it's just a little wet, you can add a shovel of dry sand, one-third of a shovel of lime, and one-quarter shovel of Portland. If it's real wet, you might need three shovels of sand, one of lime and two-thirds of a shovel of Portland. (In that case, you really put in way too much water at the outset; be cautious with the water on the first batch of each day.) When the mix is a little dry, but almost right, add a very small quantity of water. When you're close, a little water makes a huge difference. Hey, you'll learn! After the first day, you'll have it down pat.

We did use some alternative mixes at Stoneview, to give students some options, particularly the use of commercial cement retarder instead of sawdust and the use of lime putty mortar.

Cement Retarder

When favorable kinds of sawdust are not available, or if your test batch is not performing as you would like (the

Fig. 6.2: *Darin Roy mixes a batch of cordwood mortar.*

NEAL PRESSLEY

mortar shrinks and cracks), you can make mortar without the sawdust, and, instead, add a small quantity of one of the commercially available cement retarders. I have had good success with Daratard-17 from W.R. Grace Construction Products Division and also Plastiment™ from Sika Corporation. We have found that about three ounces of either of these liquid retarders works well with a wheelbarrow of mortar. The time to add the retarder is right after you put the first splash of water in the crater. Add the retarder to the water in the crater and swirl it around with the hoe.

Do not combine the wet sawdust method with the cement retarder. Leave the sawdust out altogether and increase the amount of sand by one shovelful to make up the missing bulk. So, introduce the materials into the barrow using this slightly different cadence:

- 3 sand, 1 lime, 1 Portland
- 4 sand, 1 lime, 1 Portland
- 3 sand, 1 lime

In terms of moisture, density and plasticity, you are looking for the same "stone mortar" as described above. Use the same snowball test.

We actually used some batches of "retarder mix" at Stoneview, just to show students how to do it. The performance is about the same. With both mortars, you can scratch Monday's work on Tuesday — and quite easily — with just your fingernail. On Wednesday, you can still scratch it, but not so easily. By Thursday, you may not be able to scratch Monday's mortar with your fingernail at all.

In cold weather (naturally slow-setting conditions), you should cut the amount of retarder (or wet sawdust) by half.

Lime Putty Mortar

In 1824, British stone mason Joseph Aspdin patented a cement that he made from finely ground limestone and clay, and heated in his kitchen stove. Prior to Aspdin's "Portland cement" — it resembled stone quarried on the Isle of Portland — masons used a lime-based mortar, dating back to Roman and

Mayan times. Many "natural" and "green" builders object to Portland cement because of its high "embodied energy;" that is, it takes a lot of energy to make the stuff. In fact, my friend and green building author Dan Chiras tells us that "the cement industry is one of the largest producers of carbon dioxide in the United States ... Worldwide, manufacture of cement is responsible for eight percent of all carbon dioxide emissions." Catherine Wanek, another friend and natural building author, told me that "Portland cement also releases CO_2 while it is curing, whereas lime actually pulls CO_2 out of the atmosphere as it cures." I certainly can't argue with my esteemed friends.

We have been experimenting with lime putty mortar for the past three years, and with good success. We even built an entire panel with lime putty mortar at Stoneview. We liked working with it, how it performed, and its appearance. Our neighbors recently built an entire cordwood home with lime putty mortar.

Lime putty mortar consists of sand, lime and water. That's it. But the lime needs to be hydrated for at least three days prior to using it. Listen:

Pour water into an open-topped waterproof vessel to 40 percent (two-fifths) of its capacity. (My neighbors like a 55-gallon plastic barrel cut into two cylindrical tubs.) Add bags of Type S builder's lime (agricultural lime does not work!) and mix it into the water until the so-called "lime putty" has the consistency of a very thick milkshake (*not* glazing putty.) You can mix it in with a broom handle, but what really works well is a heavy mixing attachment on a sturdy hand-held electric drill. The mixing is much easier and takes about ten percent of the time it takes to stir by hand. (Tip: Don't switch the drill on until the mixer is fully submerged, or lime putty will fly all over the place. Turn it off in there, too!) My drill and mixing attachment are seen in Figure 6.3.

Let the lime putty hydrate for at least three days. It will keep indefinitely as long as there is a film of water over the top, because lime chemically sets with the carbon dioxide in the air, (not water, as with Portland cement.)

We have arrived at a preferred ratio of 2½ parts sand to one part of lime putty, parts measured by volume, not weight. As you can't readily ladle out

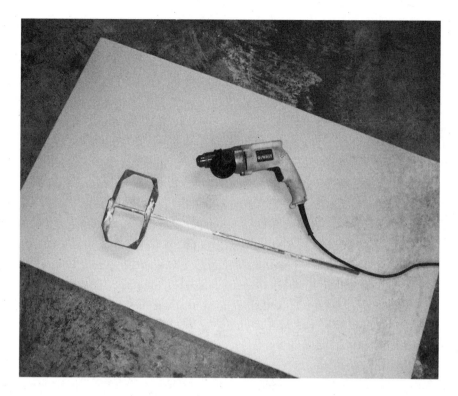

Fig. 6.3: *A stout electric drill with a paddle mixer like this one really cuts down on the labor of making lime putty.*

"shovelfuls" of lime putty, you will need a volume measure. We use two plastic pails, a two-gallon one for the lime putty and a five-gallon pail for the sand. And we have discovered that mixing time is lessened if you first put about half the sand in the wheelbarrow, then all the lime putty, and then mix it. You will soon get a homogenous wet mix. Then add the other half of the sand and mix it in. Very often, the resulting mix is pretty close to the consistency that you are looking for, which is the same as the other mortars described above. The major difference is that the mix will be even more plastic.

In practice, with a standard contractor's wheelbarrow, I will put a full five-gallon pail of sand into the barrow, make a bit of a depression in the middle of it, and add two 2-gallon pails of the lime putty. We mix it with a hoe until we have a constant color and consistency. It will be quite wet. Then we add the second five-gallon pail of sand and mix it in with the hoe. A little extra water may be necessary to get a good snowball test. It is important to keep your sand pile covered and fairly dry, as we have found. If you follow the 2.5:1 ratio with wet sand, you might not be able to get a stiff enough mortar.

Use lime putty just as you would use a cement-based mortar. Besides greater plasticity, the major difference you will notice is that you may not be able to point it as soon. Because of the slow curing rate of lime putty mortar, our neighbors would lay the log-ends one day, and point it the next day. We have found that it is possible to point the walls even three days later.

The advantages of lime putty mortar are: (1) It uses just sand and lime, no cement or retarding agent; (2) It is very plastic and cohesive to work with, never crumbly; (3) It's much more environmentally friendly than cement mortar; (4) It cracks less than cement-mortars, and small cracks can reseal themselves over time by continued calcification; (5) It has a long track record. Some Roman mortars are still hard and strong after 2,000 years; (6) It is very light in color; (7) And there is no rush on the pointing, although I do advise doing it by the next day at least, otherwise you are upsetting the mortar's attempt at setting.

Disadvantages are: (1) In some parts of the country, Type S lime is hard to find. *But it is there*. Ask local masons where they get it; (2) It varies a great deal in price around the country. In northern New York, lime putty mortar is cheaper than cement-based mortar, but in the South, it might be more expensive; (3) You need to hydrate the lime for at least three days ahead of time, but this just takes a little planning; (4) Full mortar strength — or nearly full strength — may take a month; (5) It is much messier to work with, gets on clothing, creeps up tools, etc.; (6) Because of its slow set, it is subject to frost damage for a much longer period of time, say three or four weeks instead of a couple of days for cement mortar.

Jaki and I like the lime putty mortar, but have not completely converted yet. Both mortars are performing well, and it may be another few years before we have enough results for a more definitive opinion. Early returns are promising. If you have a big problem with Portland cement, you should go for the lime mortar for peace of mind. I don't like cars and jet planes for environmental reasons, but I still use them. "Awareness and moderation in all things" generally works pretty well.

I have taken time to discuss and describe lime mortar, because I have not covered the subject in any of my other mass-market books.

The Sawdust Insulation

The late great Jack Henstridge taught me many years ago that sawdust is a highly effective, low-cost, easy to install insulation for use in the space between the inner and outer mortar joints of a cordwood wall. We get our sawdust by the pickup truckload and pass it through a half-inch mesh screen to remove the bark and other various flotsam and jetsam that finds its way into the sawdust pile. Then we mix the sawdust in an old wheelbarrow at the ratio of 12 parts of sawdust to 1 part Type S hydrated lime, the same stuff you use in your mortar. A good way to do this is to put six shovelfuls of sawdust into the barrow, then a shovel of lime, then six more shovels of sawdust. The lime is in the middle of the load now, like the cream filling of a cupcake. With a hoe, simply mix the ingredients until you have a consistent color throughout. Use dry — not soaked — sawdust, but if it is too dry and inclined to blow around onto the adjacent mortar joints, you may need to spray it with water and remix, until you cut down on this "dusting." Lime is not pleasant or healthy to ingest, so it is good to wear a facemask when mixing, as with the mortar.

Key Pieces

Cordwood masonry is strong on compression, but not very strong on tension, because of the weak bond between wood and mortar. Compartmentalizing the masonry within a post and beam makes the wall much stronger against lateral pressure, such as oscillation during a seismic event. However, we can further improve the lateral strength by mechanically locking the cordwood into the panel. With Method One and Method Two posts, discussed in Chapter 1, we nail or screw a 1-inch by 2½-inch wooden "key piece" to the side of the post, corresponding to the center third of the post's width. The

Fig. 6.4: *The key piece on the right is fastened to the 2-by-4 spacer used with a Method Three octagon post. The key piece on the left is fastened to the center third of a 2-by-8 window frame.*

key piece can be made of scrap material and installed in pieces as short as a few inches. Run the key from the foundation right to the underside of the girt. To key a Method Three post, see Figure 6.4.

A Method Four post, built up of four pieces of increasingly wide two-bys, does not require a key piece. The sawtoothed edge locks the mortar to the post.

We use key pieces on the sides of door and window frame to help lock these frames into the cordwood panel. We do not use keys on the tops or bottoms of window frames, where the key pieces get in the way of easy placement of the frame. You can see how to "lock" a window frame into a cordwood panel if you jump ahead to Figure 6.17.

Some builders have tried to tie the cordwood mortar to the framework with bent nails fastened to the posts or window frames. This has not been a success. When — not *if* — the frame shrinks away from the mortar, the bent nails will truly grab the mortar as intended, but this creates a ragged tear in the mortar, one vertical course back from the post or frame.

This key piece is important, and can be installed quickly and cheaply by using scrap. Prep the whole frame before commencing cordwood work. Put key pieces on the mortar sides of door and window frames, too.

Building the Cordwood Wall

We began building cordwood walls right on Stoneview's floating slab. In very wet climates, it would probably be a good idea to mortar up a course of eight-inch concrete blocks first, to keep the cordwood further off the ground. We actually did this with eight-inch cordwood on a 24-foot square post and beam home on the wet (east) side of Big Island Hawaii. In damp climates like that, you should probably keep your posts eight inches off the slab, as well, or use pressure-treated posts, sealed on the interior.

Most of the cordwood work at Stoneview was done by students, with Jaki and me keeping a fairly strict eye on the project to maintain what I call "build quality." It looks like one mason could have built the guesthouse. We provide each pair of students with one of our non-patented "MIM" guide sticks made from one-by-three or one-by-four, and seen in Figure 6.5. MIM stands for: Mortar, Insulation,

Fig. 6.5: *The MIM stick is used as a guide for new builders to gauge their mortar width. If you make it from full one-inch stock, it can also double as a gauge for the depth of mortar.*

Mortar. For an eight-inch wall, each mortar joint has a width of 2½ inches. The sawdust insulation gap is also 2½ inches. Three times 2½ equals 7½ inches. The other half-inch is split up between the cordwood reveal on both the inside and outside of the wall. We describe the wood as being a quarter inch "proud" of the mortar background. This reveal occurs during the laying up of the mortar and is further refined during pointing, described below.

The mantra is: "Mortar, Insulation, Wood." Sticking to this order of things — and handling just one material at a time — is the best way to develop speed; and speed is important, because cordwood masonry can be time-consuming if done inefficiently.

The first course. Clean the concrete slab of dust with a damp brush. Then, using cloth lined rubber gloves, not a trowel, place a 2½-inch wide by 1-inch thick mortar joint on the foundation. Keep the "mud" about an inch back from the edge of the slab, like the posts are. We find that with small joints like these, it is possible to grab about the right size of mortar glob with each hand, and place them one right after the other. Once you get the knack of this hand-over-hand technique, the mortar placement goes very quickly indeed. Check your work with the MIM stick. Are the mortar joints too narrow? (This is a common error.) Are they too thick or too thin? (About an inch in thickness is good.) When you are first learning, run this double bed of mortar — inner and outer beds — for three or four feet. Later, with experience, you'll be able to run the mortar from post to post, about eight feet. Put a little mortar up the side of the post slightly, about an inch thick. With "stone mortar," you can build three or four inches up the post without the mortar slumping. Rubbing the post first with a little mortar helps it to adhere.

Next, following the mantra, install the sawdust. We use a two-gallon plastic pail with a little pour spout on the rim. Move the bucket back and forth along the same line as the mortar. Tilt the bucket and shake it very slightly until the sawdust insulation begins to flow. Keep the bucket moving, so that you are applying the insulation slowly and steadily to the cavity. Keep pouring, moving along the section you're working, until a nice little raised ridge of insulation is showing slightly above the top of the mortar joints, as per Figure 6.6.

It is good to have two or three different sizes of tin can handy for placing insulation. Sometimes the bucket is too cumbersome for areas close to a post, or other awkward spaces. Bend the tin can slightly to create a good pouring spout or lip.

Mortar and insulation are installed on the first course. Now it's time for the wood — the log-ends. As previously stated, we used a variety of different sizes of cedar rounds. It is important to deplete your stock of log-ends in a consistent way. It's tempting to lay down a course of similar sized log-ends — all of about six inches diameter, for example — because it is so fast and easy. And the next course will go real fast, too, as you just half-lap the first course like bricks. But, unless six-inch logs are all you've got, you'll soon run out of that size, and then, as the song goes, there's trouble in River City.

When you have a variety of sizes to choose from, it is a good strategy to deliberately get the wall into what we call the "random rubble" style right on the first course. This is easy to do, because virtually any log-ends will work on the first course. So we try to impart a "randomness" in our selection of diameters for the first course of logs, for example: 4-inch, 6-inch, 3-inch, 3-inch, 8-inch, 5-inch, 6-inch, 4-inch, 8-inch. You get the idea.

Fig. 6.6: Top: Loose sawdust insulation can be left a bit high in the middle. Bottom: The log-end will push the sawdust into the voids either side of the raised ridge.

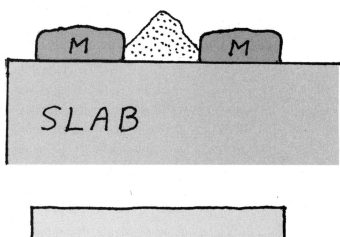

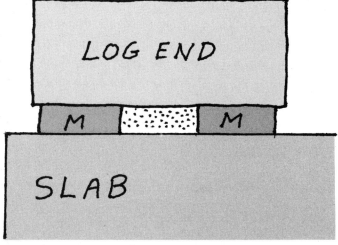

Set the first log-end up against the mortar that you placed next to the post. In fact, the center third of the log-end can actually touch the key piece here. If you use true inch-wide key pieces, they will serve as a spacer to give the correct width of mortar joints near posts (or window or door frames.) You don't have to press the log-end hard, or hammer it. Just set it into the mortar with a gentle vibrating motion, creating a slight "suction bond." You can feel this bond if you gently try to lift the log-end off of the mortar.

Over the years, we have learned another little efficiency tip, particularly useful with fairly narrow walls and small mortar joints like those at Stoneview. It is this: After you lay the first log-end, immediately place a small handful of mortar "mud" up against it, at both the inner and outer mortar joints. Now you are ready to place the second log-end. (Remember to "think random.") Now, it *is possible* to place all the log-ends down on the first course, keeping an inch space between them, and then fill the spaces between logs after with mortar, but it can be quite cumbersome to get this mud into the small spaces of an eight-inch wall. It is quicker and easier to place the mud up against the previous log-end before installing the next one. This tip only slightly compromises the efficiency goal of handling just one material at a time.

The second course ... is a little different from the first, but, once again, we want to handle just one kind of material as much as possible. This time, we run the mortar along the little hills and valleys established by the random selection of the first course, including what Jaki and I call "filling the teeth" (installing mud) between log-ends. Then we use our bucket and tin cans to pour the sawdust insulation between the mortar joints. This time, we use the fingers of our gloved hands to tamp the sawdust into the gaps between log-ends, which prevents settling of sawdust — and voids — later on.

The very act of placing the mortar and insulation at a fairly consistent one-inch thickness establishes a number of "cradles" in the mortar, which aid in the selection of log-ends. We say that "the wall begins to build itself." The builder simply looks at the size and shape of a particular cradle and then selects a log-end of similar size and shape. If the log rolls around in the cradle, it is too small. If it won't fit in, it is too big. See Figures 6.8 and 6.9.

Pointing

Pointing is the process of smoothing the mortar between log-ends. Also called grouting, pointing is a very important part of cordwood masonry, to wit:

1 A good stiff pressure with the pointing tool (described below) maximizes the friction bond between wood and mortar.

2 Pointing makes the wall look good. A poorly laid — but nicely pointed — panel actually looks better than a well-built wall that's not pointed (or poorly pointed.) So build well and point well, and you'll have a tight and beautiful wall.

3 Pointing smoothens the wall, making the mortar more water-repelling on the outside and less dusty on the inside.

4 Recessing the mortar (finally accomplished during pointing) makes it easier to conduct a repair if, say, the mortar or the wood shrinks later on. And recessed pointing gives a pleasing masonry texture.

We make pointing knives from old non-serrated butter knives, often found at garage sales and thrift stores. Bend the last inch of the knife to about a 15-degree angle, so that you can get the tip near the mortar without your gloved hand hitting the wall. Make several pointing knives of varying widths: say 3/8 inch to a full inch. You'll soon find a favorite, and the smaller ones are useful for tight spaces.

Jaki, pointer extraordinaire, does a "rough pointing" first with her rubber gloves. She removes excess mortar and catches it in her hand. Then, with her gloved fingers or the pointing knife, she presses the excess into voids. This can be done quite soon after laying the mortar and wood.

The finished pointing is generally done as soon as a half hour after laying a Portland-based mortar (on hot, dry days) or as late as 90 to 120 minutes later on cool damp days, when the mortar sets much more slowly. (Lime putty mortar can be pointed the same day or the next day ... or, sometimes, even the day after that!)

Fig. 6.7: *The mortar is tightened, recessed and smoothed by applying firm pressure with a pointing knife.*

Press quite hard with the knife blade, while drawing the mortar out smoothly with a side-to-side or down-to-up movement. Try to smoothen out the knife marks. Do not over-point (or point too early), which brings excess moisture to the surface, which, in turn, will cause mortar shrinkage cracking.

Pointing is time-consuming, but important. Decide on a degree of finish that suits you, and stick with it. Any pointing is better than none at all.

Tricks of the Trade

Here are some other cordwood building tips to keep in mind, culled over 30 years of experience:

1   *Maintain constant mortar spacing* between adjacent log-ends, about an inch or so. Avoid the three- to four-inch trap, where you can't get any log-end in the space.

2   *Cover vertical mortar joints with another log-end.* Masons say, "one over two, two over one." Obviously, there is a continuous vertical joint near the posts, but the key piece locks the cordwood masonry to the frame very well at the panel's edges.

3   *Balance sizes and shapes.* We make an effort on the first course to get into the random rubble look. But the wall sometimes gets lazy — or is it the builder? — and falls back into a pattern of using too many of a particular size. We tell students to stand back ten feet from the wall occasionally and critique their own work. If an unwanted pattern (too many log-ends the same) is developing, make a conscious effort to break out of it.

4   *Eyeball from post to post* to see if the cordwood wall is plumb. You can adjust today's log-ends in and out with a hammer to maintain plumb. You can't safely move yesterday's work, unless you are using lime putty mortar. If posts are rounded and you can't get a good sight line, frequent use of the plumb bubble on a four-foot level will keep the wall going up straight. Stoneview's relatively small panels make keeping the cordwood masonry plumb a fairly easy matter. But keep an eye out for bowing of the wall ("wowing" in Canada), and correct it as needed.

5   *Cover cement-based mortars quickly.* When you place mortar down, get in the habit of installing the insulation right away, and then covering the mortar joint with your logs. Don't place mortar down and then wander off for lunch or even to make a batch. When you return, the mud may be already stiff and difficult to set a log into. On this same note, finish the day's work with wood, not mortar on top of wood, which will result in a "double-thick" mortar joint when you return to that section the next day.

Step 1, Mortar.

Step 2, Sawdust.

Step 3, Log-end.

Step 4, A little more mortar.

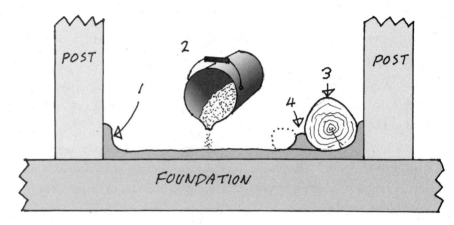

Fig. 6.8: *First course. Continue alternating steps 2, 3 and 4 until the first course is complete.*

The exception is that you finish with mortar if it completes the panel up to the girt.

6 *Finishing for the day.* Leave flat full-width mortar joints between log-ends to support the next day's mortar. Don't leave a chamfered or sloped edge on the mortar, as this will not provide adequate bearing for the next day.

7 *Work the valleys.* After a little while, your cordwood courses will have high and low parts, what we call hills and valleys. Always work in the valleys first, which create new hills … and new valleys. Log-ends need support from their fellows. If you build on the hills or build too high in an area, it is hard to get the needed support. See Figure 6.9, next page.

Now let's look at some of the special features that can make cordwood so personal and so much fun.

Bottle-Ends

We did a lot of bottle-ends at Stoneview, 121 to be precise. Most of them — but not all — are part of planned groupings. We think that a good part of the building's magical charm comes from the use of color and pattern in various deliberately planned panels.

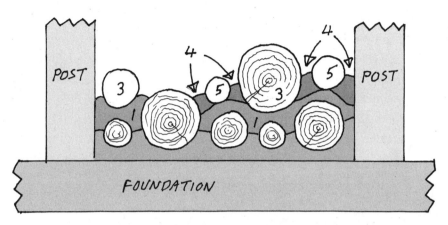

Fig. 6.9: *Second and subsequent courses.*

Step 1, Mortar, including "filling teeth" of first course.

Step 2, Install insulation (not shown).

Step 3, Install log-ends in "valleys."

Step 4, "Cradle" for more log-ends.

Step 5, Fill cradles with more log-ends, then start over at Step 1.

The cordwood walls at Stoneview are all eight inches thick. Bottle-ends can be up to a half-inch longer, as the bases of bottles and jars often have a quarter-inch chamfered edge. We point the mortar up to the basic cylinder and let the extra quarter inch extend a little more proud of the wall. We save useful bottles and jars from household use, but two other good sources are (1) the local recycling center, where, often, the bottles are already sorted by color and (2) your local tavern, where they have a very interesting selection of bottles in a variety of shapes and colors. They are glad to have you haul a few cases away. Remember that you need a clear bottle or jar to match with each colored one. Remove all labels by soaking for a few hours, and clean the inside of the bottles with hot soapy water. Rinse, and set to dry.

There are two basic ways to create 8- to 8½-inch bottle-ends: Cutting bottles, or plugging the necks of bottles into a glass vessel, such as salsa, baby food or olive jar.

Cutting bottles: Over the years, we have tried a number of different ways of cutting bottles. Most methods are difficult or messy and have a success ration of between 50 and 80 percent. Since 2000, we have become enamored of a very easy, precise and safe method, and one having a success ratio of about 95 percent. I won't waste the reader's time with the other methods.

We bought a power tool called a slate and tile cutter at out local Lowe's home improvement store, for just under $100. We wish we'd bought one years ago. The tool is essentially a small table saw with a rotating six-inch diamond-tipped blade extending above the table. The bottom half of the blade is constantly cooled and lubricated because it passes through an inch of water in a tub below the table surface. The normal purpose for this tool is to cut ceramic tiles or slates, and I've used ours for these purposes. But it is also the best tool for cutting bottles. You can see it in Figure 6.10. We set the fence

Fig. 6.10: *Cutting a bottle with a slate and tile cutter.*

so that it is 4 to 4¼ inches from the edge of the blade. Start the saw. If there is too much water splashing all over, stop the saw and pour some water out. The blade needs to stay wet, that's all. Then, wearing cloth-lined rubber gloves and eye protection, hold the bottle firmly with two hands, one on the barrel and one on the neck. Turn the bottle into the blade one full revolution. Use the fence as a guide stop. The bottle will break off cleanly when you get back to the point of beginning.

Handle the fresh cut glass with care. Rinse the "tumblers" you have made and set them in the sun to dry. Later, choose two tumblers of similar diameter (one colored and one clear, or two clears) and simply duct tape them together into an 8- to 8½-inch bottle-end.

We then puncture the duct tape near the join with three or four holes, so that the bottle-end can "breathe" into the insulated mortar joint. If the bottle-end is sealed too well, there is a slight chance of pressure build-up in the bottle-end, which could cause cracking of the glass. This happened to two or three of our bottle-ends back in the 1970s when we tried to seal them too well. Since we began to let them breathe, none have cracked, out of several hundred that we have installed. The completed bottle end is seen in Figure 6.11.

Fig. 6.11: *A completed bottle-end. You can use a MIM stick to gauge length.*

Using clear jars and small bottles. Find a necked bottle, about eight inches long, colored or clear, and plug its neck into a clear jar of about the same diameter. Duct-tape the two pieces together, and puncture the tape a few times to let the bottle-end breathe into the insulated space. The necks of the bottles don't show at all on the interior and are hardly noticed on the exterior of the wall.

With either method of making bottle-ends, we use clear glass on the outside and colored glass on the inside. Most of the time, you want to enjoy the vibrant color from the interior. If you install them "backwards," the color is very much diffused through the bottle-end and not as attractive. You can also tape two clear jars together, if the length works out. We use a few clear bottle-ends in the patterns.

The jar method is quick and easy, as you don't have to cut bottles. You will need lots of the right size of both jars and bottles, however, so grab and stockpile them whenever you can. I buy my beer by the inch.

Designs. The odd bottle-end by itself is visually underwhelming. Bottles are best used in combination: randomly (like a constellation of stars), or as part of a deliberate purpose or pattern. At Stoneview, each panel has a different motif, and a page in the color section is devoted to some of these. As with log-ends, "planned randomness" is effective, although now there is the added dimension of color, to go along with size and shape. Take care to maintain a kind of balance — whatever it is that you perceive that to be — but be creative.

We have used old glass insulators, cat-shaped (red and blue) wine bottles, champagne glasses and other special pieces in the Stoneview walls. Two large hollow cedar logs, one each side of the door, have light blue square Sapphire gin bottles in the hollow portion.

Log-End Patterns

We made design features out of special log-ends that found their way onto the site. A timber framer gave me a quantity of 4-by-4 and 6-by-6 samples of cypress and yellow pine, all conveniently eight inches long. We made special patterns of these samples, as seen in Figures 6.12, 6.13 and 6.14. We used

Fig. 6.12: *This diamond pattern is pre-made on a bench and installed in one piece. Note snowblocking detail above girt, made from 6-by-6 wooden blocks.*

Fig. 6.13: *Students point the exterior of a large diamond pattern, which was laid out on the cardboard pattern fastened to the girt. In its down position, it serves as a guide for the placement of special log-ends and constant one-inch mortar joints.*

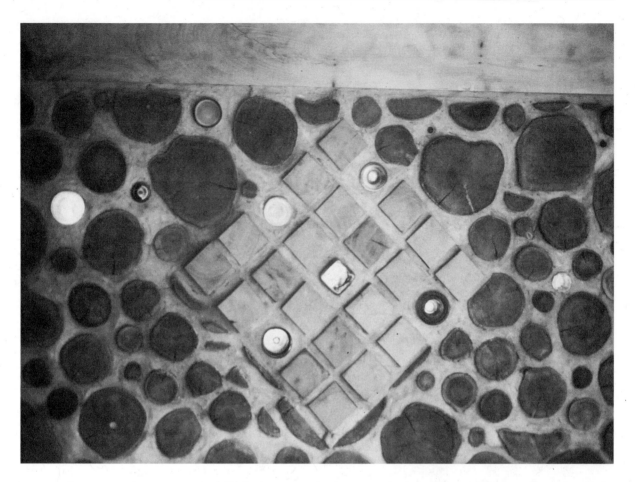

Fig. 6.14: *The completed diamond is made from 25 elements in a 5-by-5 grid, 20 log-ends and five bottle-ends.*

cut-offs from our Method One and Method Two posts to create a kind of a flower pattern, as per Figure 6.15. A mushroom appears in one of the panels, above a lovely piece of cedar laid horizontally in the wall (with a companion on the exterior). These features can be seen in the color section. Twin baby dragons showed one day while I was cutting hardwood firewood, the result of mottled wood discoloration, also seen in the color section. We say they were born of the egg above them. One log-end is almost the exact shape of the island of Moorea in French Polynesia, where we once spent 11 happy days. The log-end even suggests the coral reef which surrounds the

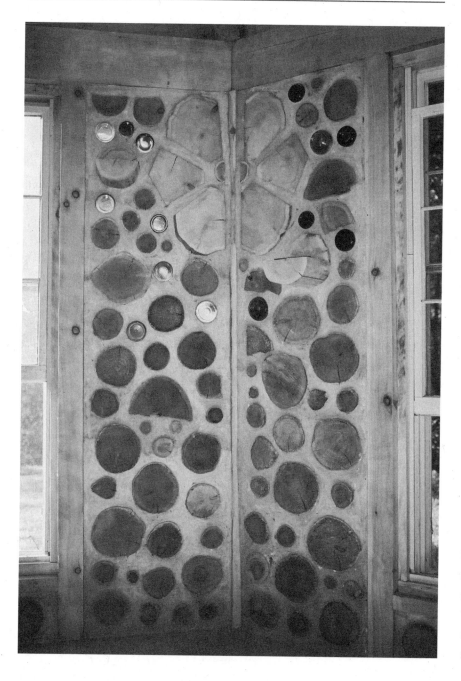

Fig. 6.15: *In this flower design, four of the six log-ends made from Method One and Method Two posts were screwed to the wall before the cordwood masonry commenced.*

Fig. 6.16: *The beautiful tropical island of Moorea is captured in this polished log-end.*

island. We have placed tropical features, including "Pacific lagoon" green bottle-ends around this special varnished log-end.

Window Frames

Three of the four large double-hung windows — and the door — are framed on their right and left sides by 4-by-8 timbers, floor to girt, as described in Chapter 4. All that remained, with the windows, was to measure for and install a windowsill piece. We made our sills of 2-by-8 planking, and you can see it in several pictures in this book. To figure the window's rough opening, add a half-inch of clearance to both the height and the width of the window's own frame. We had two different sizes of windows, and made corresponding rough openings for each. Because the windows were quite large, it turned out that there was only ten inches of space beneath one of the windowsills, and seven inches beneath the three slightly larger ones. We did random rubble cordwood in the large space, and used a single course of 5- to 5½-inch cedar rounds beneath the larger ones. The sills were placed right on top of the cordwood and fastened to the 4-by-8 frames with a couple of small GRK finish screws, toe-screwed to the frame.

The crank-out casement window in the bathroom was much smaller. We made its frame of two-by-eights and screwed it right to the underside of the girt. Again, the rough opening is a half inch greater than the window, both

Fig. 6.17: *A window frame can "float" in a cordwood panel. Note key piece on the side of the frame.*

height and width. We were careful to maintain plumb with bracing until the frame was surrounded with cordwood. Also, we installed 1-inch by 2½-inch key pieces to the sides of the frame that would be against the cordwood masonry, further locking it in place. We installed a frame for the smallest of the four large windows in the same way, and it can be seen back in Figure 4.19. Figure 6.17 shows a "floating" window frame in Bruce Kilgore's 16-sided cordwood cabin.

Finishing near the Top

As cordwood masonry begins to get close to the underside of the girt, you can start to plan the log-ends for the final fit. Ideally, you want to finish with the same one-inch mortar joint at the top as you have on the sides and the bottom of the pile. A time-proven method of doing this is to nail or screw a piece of 1-inch by 2½-inch Styrofoam® insulation to the entire underside of the girt and then to fit the log-ends tight up against this piece of insulation. You can get a nearly perfect fit by careful selection, but sometimes it may be necessary to hold a clear-grained log-end up to the space and mark it with a pencil so that, when split, it will fit perfectly. Mark it and stand it on a chopping block. Place an axe on the pencil mark and give the flat end of the axe-head a good swift hit with a sledgehammer. *Wear eye protection when hitting metal with metal!* The resulting piece will fit the designated spot perfectly.

To easily fill in the last mortar joint, load the back of a mason's or plasterer's trowel with a handful of mortar and hold it up to the gap to be filled. Then, with a pointing knife, push the mortar off the back of the trowel and hard up against the Styrofoam® insulation, which provides resistance.

Sometimes it is difficult to install the insulation on the last couple of courses of cordwood masonry. Even a small can might be hard to fit in the space for the purpose of pouring sawdust. One way of attending to this detail is to make a channeling tool of light metal flashing or even cardboard. This tool might be ten inches long and four inches wide, crimped down its length to form a shallow trough. Place the sawdust on one end of the tool and then vibrate the material along the trough so that it falls into the insulated gap in the middle of the wall. Another method is to stuff in clumps of fiberglass insulation into the spaces between the last couple of mortar joints. Eye and nose protection *must* be used when handling raw fiberglass. Try to fill all the voids. The fiberglass, like the Styrofoam® at the top of the panel, provides good resistance when you press mortar up against it.

Snowblocking ...

... is what we call the infilling between rafters, from the girt to the underside of the planking. There are 16 such panels to fill in at Stoneview. This can be

Fig. 6.18: *Jaki and Darin used bottle-ends and even a pair of nautilus fossils to liven up the snowblocking above the door.*

a potentially awkward detail to do with cordwood masonry, although Jaki and son Darin did a nice job of it on the two snowblocking panels over the door, as seen in Figure 6.18. It is much easier to do ordinary cordwood in this area before the planking goes on, so that you can get at the work from above. Just screed the top mortar joint with a good straight edge, such as a piece of two-by-four, and point right up to that edge. Otherwise, the work is much like that in "Finishing near the Top," above.

At Stoneview, we used a much easier method of finishing snowblocking detail, by making use of a number of leftover logs from our local log home company. These pieces were milled three sides, with one side left in its original rounded edge log configuration. The pieces are uniformly 6¾ inches thick. Scraps of four-by-six, six-by-six, or six-by-eight would all do nicely, too, as would leftover pieces of rafters or girts, although the installation would be a little different. Ten of our salvaged pieces were long enough to fill in snowblocking panels, and we did two more panels by using two shorter pieces end to end.

The part of the girt upon which the snowblocking will be placed is trapezoidal in shape. Where the middle rafter of any side intersects the girt, this trapezoid has a square end, making a "right trapezoid."

Making snowblocks. First, we trimmed one end of the snowblock to a right angle, if it didn't already have one. Then we measured the long side of the trapezoid along the girt, usually about 46 inches. We subtracted three inches from the measured length and marked the top or bottom of the snowblock and made a pencil mark, say 43 inches from the right-angled end. Then, with an angle square, we marked the top (or bottom) of the snowblock with a line heading back from our pencil mark at a 22.5-degree angle, giving some shorter measure for the inner side, say 41 inches. We cut along this mark with a chainsaw.

We nailed 1- by 2-inch pieces of Styrofoam Blueboard® to the top of the snowblock and to each end, keeping the rigid foam in the center third of the piece. Had we used 6-by-6 material for snowblocks, we could have installed a similar piece of Styrofoam® to its underside as well, but our log cabin

pieces were 6¾ inches thick. As rafters were 7¾ inches high, we just had room for foam on the top, and let the snowblock's underside bear right on the girt. Besides insulating the mortar, yet to come, the Styrofoam® also assists in jamming the snowblock tightly into the space. The curved surface is in the same plane as the outside wall, while there is a two-inch "shelf" on the girt, as seen from the inside. See Figures 6.19, 6.20 and 6.21.

The snowblocks are quickly installed. After jamming them in place, the mortar can be pushed off of the back of a trowel into the roughly 1- by 2-inch gap, as described in the previous section, "Finishing near the Top."

Fig. 6.19: *Log cabin scraps make excellent snowblocking, mortared on three sides.*

Fig. 6.20: *Although it looks like a square post, this is actually the exterior surface of a Method Four octagon post made up of a two-by-two, two-by-four, two-by-six, and a two-by-eight (shown), and described in Chapter 4. Note the log cabin piece, loose in the snow-block area.*

Because of the trapezoidal snowblock's draft angle, it is best to mortar the outside first, then the inside.

We ran out of the log cabin pieces for the last two snowblocks in the bathroom area, but used up some leftover 6-by-6 yellow pine timber samples as seen back in Figure 6.12. These samples, each about eight inches long, are surrounded by 1- by 2-inch pieces of Dow Styrofoam®, for insulation and to assist in jamming them in place until the mortar is installed. These panels look nice, too. There are all kinds of ways to put scrap to good use.

Extra rafter material can be used as good tight-fitting snowblocking, without the mortar. Measuring and cutting have to be fairly precise. In the next chapter, you'll see that we did something like that internally over the bathroom door. You'll need about 64 linear feet of this. As you really shouldn't have that much "waste," you might consider ordering extra 4-by-8 material — or even six-by-eight or eight-by-eight — for the purpose.

That's the essential info on cordwood. For a more thorough look at the technique, see *Cordwood Building: The State of the Art* (New Society, 2003) or the 195-minute *Complete Cordwood DVD* (Earthwood Building School, distributed by New Society, 2007.) Or come to a cordwood masonry workshop at Earthwood. You can stay at Stoneview while you're here!

Fig. 6.21: *On the interior, there is a two-inch shelf on the girt, because the 6-inch-wide snowblocks are held to the exterior.*

Windows and Door

C hapter 6 was long and important. Chapter 7 will be short … but just as important.

Recycled Door and Windows at Stoneview

People spend a lot of money on windows and doors, especially on new homes, where these items can approach 20 percent of the total materials cost. And then the *mortgage* (from the French, meaning "death pledge") compounds the error for 20 years or more. This is ridiculous and unnecessary.

Economy of construction benefits from making good use of indigenous and recycled materials. Jaki and I noticed an ad in the paper for five large Andersen double-hung windows for sale, with insulated glass and screens. We called the owner to get directions and drove nearly two hours to look at the windows. The friendly owner had replaced all of the windows in his sun room with new ones, although the old white vinyl-clad Andersens were still in pretty good condition, just a couple of minor flaws in the vinyl. Three were 42 by 69 inches and two were 38 by 65 inches. Mullions subdivided the glass into 20 "lites" for the large ones, 16 lites for the smaller ones. We bought the lot for $250.

The door was one of a pair of French doors that Bruce Kilgore had been given at work. As he had no immediate use for them, he offered them to us. I gave one to a neighbor who actually used it as a tilt-up window in his new cordwood garden shed, and Jaki and I used the other. The 34½- by 77½-inch door is wooden with a large pane of heavy insulated glass. Like the windows, the glass is divided by mullions into a number of smaller lites. This architectural feature unifies the door with the windows; nice, as all of the elements are in the same large room. As discussed in Chapter 4, our 6-foot 6-inch post height was a function of the (almost) 6-foot 6-inch-high door.

As we didn't need all five large windows, we sold one for $75 to someone who could make good use of it, so the windows actually cost us $175 plus the time and gas to go and fetch them. The smaller crank-out bathroom window, also thermal pane glass, was recycled from a window we took out at Earthwood when we added our new sunroom a few years ago.

Unless you have money to burn, you should never pay full retail price for doors and windows, even new ones. You can always find them at a fraction of retail in the newspaper classifieds, in bargain rooms at lumberyards, Habitat for Humanity stores, and the like. Perfectly good unused thermal pane units are always available at the "back room" of manufacturers. You'll buy them at a fraction of the cost of specially ordered units. Usually, these back room units were cut the wrong size for a job. At the design stage, you can make them work for you.

The doors and windows for your project will likely be a lot different from ours. You might spend more or less than the $175 that we spent. Comparable new units would have set us back at least $1,750.

Intern Nick Brown had been a great help to us in pad work, forming, and pouring the slab. Towards the end of the Stoneview project, another intern, Dean Koyanagi, joined us. Like Nick, Dean had come to Earthwood to learn the various building techniques that we have developed over the years. And, like Nick, Dean was a good self-motivated worker. The success of Stoneview owes a lot to these two young gentlemen, who were both like adopted sons to us by the time they departed.

Installing the Four Large Windows

Our large double-hung windows came pre-hung in their own vinyl-clad 1-by-6-inch frames. The rough opening in the timber frame is a half-inch greater in each direction than the windows' own frames. I installed the first large window with Dean, and he pretty much did the rest by himself.

My favorite stock for installing both fixed thermal pane and pre-hung windows is one-by-one-inch molding. It is cheap, easy to work with, and in keeping with the rustic style of the building. Using a circular saw, Dean and I marked and ripped one-by boards into one-by-ones. However, it is safer and easier to make one-by-one molding with a table saw, and you get a straighter smoother cut. I don't own one, but sometimes wish I did.

On the building's exterior, we let the window's own 1-by-6 frame extend an inch proud of the rough opening. This rough opening, as previously described, is composed of the girt, the 4-by-8 vertical rough framing, and the 2-by-8 sill. We friction-fit the pre-hung frame to the rough frame by jamming the roughly quarter-inch gap with tapered cedar shingles. We snugged the frame into the rough opening by using opposing tapered shingles in the same location. Gently tapping the shingles with a hammer firms the unit into its opening. Use shims every couple of feet around the window's 1-by-6 frame. We made sure that the sashes moved up and down easily, and then screwed the inner frame to the inner side of the rough opening. We always screw through shingle shims, so as not to warp the window's own pre-hung frame. We used holes in the frame that had already been used for the same purpose at their previous location. One screw on each side was sufficient to hold the frame in place until the 1-by-1-inch molding was installed on each side.

Dean actually installed all the 1-by-1 molding, inside and out, in about a day. On the outside, he would cut a piece of molding about 2½ inches longer than the width of the rough opening, and then nail it to the girt at the top. See Figure 7.1. Dean kept the molding snug against the inch of the window frame that was left proud of the timber frame. We decided not to install 1-by-1 molding to the outside of the 2-by-8 sill at the bottom, because the vinyl-clad frame had a drip edge molded into it, which we wanted to leave exposed. In fact, this was the main reason for keeping the window's own frame an inch proud of the timber frame. On the inside, top and bottom, Dean cut the pieces exactly the width of the rough opening, and installed

Fig. 7.1: *One-by-one trim pieces cover the quarter-inch gap between the pre-hung window unit and the timber frame.*

them with nails. Now the window could not move, and it only remained to measure, cut, and install the side pieces of molding. Each window, then, required seven pieces of molding, three for the outside trim, four for the inside. See also Figure 7.2.

Installing Small Windows

Our small crank-out bathroom window was installed in much the same way. The window "buck" or frame for this unit was pre-made of two-by-eights and screwed to the underside of the girt. It was held plumb with temporary bracing until the cordwood locked it into place, aided, of course, by the 1-by 2½-inch key pieces installed to both side jambs of the rough frame. Again, the rough opening of this frame is a half-inch greater in each direction than

the outside dimensions of this pre-hung unit. You would make the same allowance for a fixed thermal pane unit.

Installing the small window was very similar to installing the larger ones, except that we kept its pre-hung frame 1¼-inches back from the outside edge of the 2-by-8 window buck. We would do the same if installing fixed units of insulated glass. As there is no drip edge on this small window, four pieces of one-by-one are used on both the inside and outside to trim the window and cover the quarter-inch gap between the unit's casement and the window buck.

Fig. 7.2: *Four 1-by-1-inch trim pieces serve as low-cost rustic molding on Stoneview's interior. This is the small bathroom window.*

Installing the Door

Ours was not a pre-hung door. We'd installed the 4-by-8 doorjambs to fit our recycled door. Once again, Dean installed 1-by-1 trim (on the inside of the

Fig. 7.3: *The small crank-out bathroom window, installed.*

jambs and along the girt) as a stop for the door to close against. See Figure 7.4. The door had its own weatherstripping along the bottom.

I purchased new hinges and a doorknob, which Dean installed. The door swings perfectly and closes nicely against the trim pieces. We could install foam weather-stripping between the one-by-ones and the door for winter use, but it is a very good fit as it is.

Pre-hung doors go in very nicely, providing that you create the right rough opening in your timber frame in the first place. As with the large windows, use wooden shingles and screws (about every 20 to 24 inches) to secure the pre-hung doorframe to the timber frame. You can trim with one-by-one, or, if it is a more finished door, you may wish to buy about 40 lineal feet of an appropriate molding, to trim it inside and out.

8

Interior Finishing

I am not the right person to write how-to commentary on conventional building techniques, nor is such a discussion within the purview of this book. A clear and excellent reference on all facets of conventional building is the 704-page *Do-It-Yourself Housebuilding*, by George Nash (Sterling, 1995), and I consult it whenever I have a question about standard construction, including plumbing and electric. In the present work, I will discuss conventional building systems only as they are related to the other techniques that I have advocated over the years.

Interior Walls

Stoneview is predominantly an open-plan bedroom, dining and living area, with a separate bathroom, not unlike a hotel room. There are no kitchen facilities. See Figure 1.12, the floorplan. The bathroom is separated from the main room by ordinary 2-by-4 studded walls (16 inches on center) covered with sheetrock. The sheetrock, in turn, was taped and spackled, and covered with a primer coat and a textured finish coat. At Stoneview, intern Dean Koyanagi did the framing, and a friend, Joe Young, helped me with the sheetrock (or, rather, I helped him.)

The studded walls rise up and meet the underside of rafters, as seen in Figure 8.1. As the rafters are the same width as the depth of the studs (1½ inches), we had two choices: (1) run the sheetrock right up to the plank ceiling,

Fig. 8.1: *Some internal framing details at Stoneview.*

covering the rafters or (2) leave the ½-inch sheetrock proud of the rafters at the top by a half inch, both sides of the wall. We chose the second solution, so that we can see all of the attractive rafters heading for the building's center. Later, to finish off the top of the sheetrock, where it is proud of the wall, I purchased 24 linear feet of finished ¾-inch by ¾-inch molding and used it to trim the top of the otherwise bare sheetrock edge. It looks good, as you will see in Figure 8.2.

The framing for one wall began at the inner surface of one of our Method One posts. The framing for the other long bathroom wall met the middle of a cordwood panel, creating a useful right angle for the placement of the

square shower unit. We simply plumbed and screwed a two-by-four to the cordwood wall using 3½-inch GRK screws, and you can see it in Figure 8.1. The rafter itself, also seen in Figure 8.1, served as the top plate of the 2-by-4 frame. Not seen is a 2-by-4 floor plate, nailed to the floor using tempered concrete nails.

There is a third, shorter, bathroom wall, which encompasses the bathroom door. This wall does not rise up conveniently to meet the underside of structural rafters and it presented Dean Koyanagi with some framing challenges. The trickiest bit was to create strong framed corners where internal walls joined, and these were not right angles, as in most conventional building.

Fig. 8.2: *Sheetrock detail at the angled corner and top of wall. Fitted 4-by-8 pieces fill the spaces between rafters, above bathroom door.*

Dean figured the angles and we ripped two-by-fours on the bias to create the properly shaped built-up corner stud that would receive the sheetrock nicely.

We bought a new but inexpensive pre-hung door at the discount section of our local building supplier and framed it out as seen in Figure 8.1. Note the 2-by-4 top plate fastened to the underside of four consecutive rafters. (Only three show in the picture.) Note also that Dean carefully fitted pieces of 4-by-8 rafter scrap into the spaces between rafters. These pieces required careful measuring and angle cuts, but Dean relished this kind of challenge and did a great job. We left them exposed, as seen in Figure 8.2.

Prior to sheetrocking, we framed out for the shower cabinet and did the simple wiring, described below.

Sheetrocking. Joe Young and I measured, cut and screwed the sheetrock onto the frame in a day, Joe providing the experienced direction. We used ten sheets in all, two of them being the green "waterproof" sheetrock for use around the shower cabinet. There was nothing special about the work, except taping the roughly 135-degree corners where the short wall meets the long wall.

Jaki and I taped and spackled the sheetrock joints and screw dimples, and primed all the walls with an ivory primer. We finished with a textured paint that we made ourselves by combining four parts of joint filler compound with one part of latex paint. We applied this paint with a textured roller made for the purpose. We chose an ivory color, which is less glaring than white, but still reflects a lot of light onto the cordwood walls.

Simple Plumbing

The soakaway and waste plumbing installation was already described in Chapter 2.

Installing the base piece of the 32- by 32-inch shower was easy because we had left the drainpipe unglued in its protective box. I was able to try the base, keeping it tight against the 2-by-4 baseplate of the long internal bathroom wall and some 2-by-4 furring that we screwed to the back cordwood wall. A very small adjustment to the length and angle of my two-inch waste plumbing gave a perfect fit. I tested the shower with water, and, when I was

Cultivating Coincidences

A few years ago, novelist James Redfield wrote a bestseller called *The Celestine Prophecy*. One of the very useful lessons that can be learned from this book is his description of life as a series of intersecting synchronicities. After reading the book, I found that I was alert to all sorts of "coincidences" in my life, and others that I have discussed this with reported the same effect. In reality, the book simply makes the reader more aware and alert.

Coincidences are really a mathematical phenomenon, pure probability theory: the more events, the greater the chance of events intersecting. Coincidences are simply intersecting events, and are not mystical in any way, although they often seem so. In fact, you can create or "cultivate" coincidences. Here is just one example from Stoneview:

During the early days of construction, I was walking along our dirt road with two young couples that were both building houses in the neighborhood. I was trying to explain how coincidences could be cultivated to advantage, but wasn't breaking through to my audience. I took a chance and said, "Look, I'll give you an example of how this works. It happens that Jaki and I need a shower cabinet for Stoneview. A new shower cabinet costs 300 bucks. I mentioned my need to friends in Quebec and it turned out that they have an extra one they're not using and I can have it for the hauling. The trouble is, it's up in Quebec, two hours away. But I am mentioning our need to you folks because you might know of one closer by."

It turned out that both couples knew of shower cabinets that I could get nearby! "There," I said, matter-of-factly. "Now I've got a choice of three free shower cabinets." My friends laughed and shook their heads as if I'd pulled a rabbit out of an empty hat. All I had done was to set the laws of probability in motion, and in my favor, by expressing our need to four people. The Bible says, "Ask and you will receive." Standard wisdom says, "Nothing ventured, nothing gained." It won't always work, but if you let your need be known to enough people, somebody will be able to help.

At Stoneview, we got our shower cabinet, composting toilet, bathroom cabinet and sink, front door, floor slates, stove, and most of our cordwood by "cultivating coincidences" (letting our need be known.) The Enkadrain® and sedum for the roof came by extending ourselves to suppliers. The windows came from reading the "For Sale" ads in the paper, opening up more events.

Try it.

certain that water flowed out perfectly, dried and glued the parts. Then I framed the other short wall next to the shower. The rest of the shower cabinet came in four pieces which fasten to the shower base, to the sheetrock walls and — at the top and corners — to each other.

Our grey water goes to a soakaway instead of a septic tank, but the underfloor waste plumbing is quite conventional.

I want to share the story of how we came by the shower cabinet. Even if you never build Stoneview, the sidebar on page 167 provides a useful technique for procuring almost anything you want in life.

Our next-door neighbors remodeled their bathroom a few years ago, and replaced a small cabinet and wash-hand basin. The old one went out to their storage shed. One day, Frank told me about some old windows he wanted to get rid of, and took me to his shed. I told him that I could use the windows on a new "Mess Hall" we were building at Earthwood and asked him if the cabinet and sink were available as well. "Sure," said Frank. "We'll never use it and it's just taking space." It's perfect at Stoneview and the waste plumbing was easy to connect to the two-inch waste pipe we'd left sticking out of the slab. All I needed was a plastic reducing fitting and a flexible plastic trap. We did not make use of the faucets as you'll see a bit further on, but left them in place in case we change to a more conventional plumbing system in the future.

The Zodi System

Our neighbors, Alex and Renee, were building a cordwood house across the road. During construction, they did all their showering in an outdoor enclosure and hot water supplied by a Zodi "on-demand portable hot shower." (zodi.com) On their strong recommendation, we bought one for Stoneview, Figure 8.3. The basic unit, the Instant Hot Shower — now called a "Hot Tap" — consists of a single stainless steel on-demand propane gas heater, a base unit to hold everything steady, a six-volt water pump with debris screen, and an eight-foot hose with shower head. The pump works on four D-cell batteries, but you can get adaptors for a car battery or a conventional household electric system. Heat comes from a 16.4-ounce propane cylinder, readily available at the camping department of sporting goods stores. You also get a rugged rectangular plastic box, which doubles as a carrying case and a four-gallon water storage, enough, they say, for a ten-minute shower. The pressure is not terribly strong, but adequate. You can also get an adaptor to run the unit off of five-gallon propane barbeque tanks.

We use a five-gallon pail for the water source, which gives an extra 25 percent capacity over the plastic box supplied, and is easier to tote for refilling. We keep a 50-gallon tank of fresh water at the ready for guests outside of the building. See Figure 8.4. We fill the tank by hose from Earthwood before guests arrive. Guests can refill the pail as needed using a spigot on the bottom of the tank. Zodi offers an optional "Garden Hose Kit," which "permits unlimited use without pump/batteries."

The water can be used cold or, by igniting the piezo ignition, hot. The hose is long enough to reach either the

Fig. 8.3: *Our Zodi instant hot water system can provide a shower or can be used, as shown, for the wash-hand basin.*

shower or the wash-hand basin. We use little stainless steel spring clips to hold the hose in place. Figure 8.3 shows the hose (with its shower head) over the sink.

Zodi claims that over 60 gallons of hot water can be delivered between battery and propane tank refills. Alex and Renee said that they get about 25 showers from a 16.4-ounce propane tank. As of this writing, several guests have stayed at Stoneview and we have not yet exhausted the first propane tank, or the set of four D-cell batteries.

Other companies, including Coleman, make similar systems.

"Humanure" Toilet

Jaki and I were familiar with the sensible system of processing human waste, described in detail in our friend Joe Jenkins's excellent book *The Humanure Handbook* (see Bibliography). We'd used the system while staying at a cordwood home in northern Wisconsin, and again at our son's home in Colorado. Bruce Kilgore, too, was taken with Jenkins's methods and made an excellent humanure toilet cabinet for his own Stoneview-like

Fig. 8.4: *Bruce Kilgore provided us with this sturdy 50-gallon plastic drum, with a spigot at the bottom for filling the five-gallon pail.*

cabin nearby. I liked Bruce's cabinet so much, made from recycled wood, that I asked him if he would make one for us. He did, but warned us that he had taken some "artistic license." Wait for it.

The essence of Joe's humanure "system" is to deposit human waste into a five-gallon pail, which has been primed with a shallow layer of sawdust. (This makes dumping and cleaning the bucket easier.) After each use, the user sprinkles enough sawdust over the deposit to completely cover it — a cup or two, depending — and closes the lid of the cabinet. If the deposit is well-covered, there's no smell. When the bucket is about three-quarters full, put a tight-fitting cover on it. Joe recommends that you have at least four identical plastic buckets, with lids. When you have accumulated two buckets, carry them to a composting bin, and dump them in the middle of the pile. Joe's book tells how to make an effective, safe, animal-proof composting bin.

The Humanure Handbook also provides excellent instructions on how to make an inexpensive ($25) cabinet that will contain a bucket with a good fit.

Fig. 8.5: *Our humanure toilet cabinet is a huge cedar log-end that holds a five-gallon bucket. Note routed top surface, ready to receive a piece of fitted plywood.*

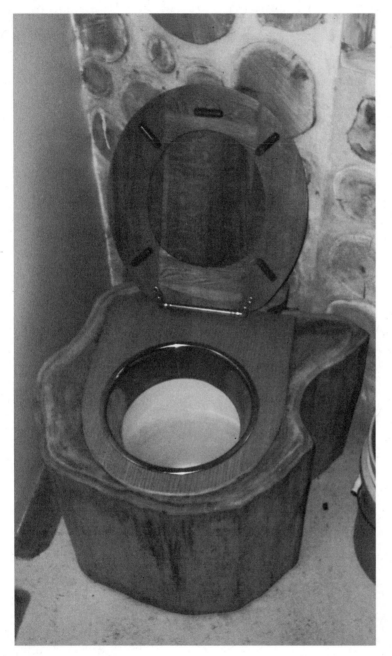

There's also a lot of information at Joe's "humanure" page at jenkinspublishing. com/humanure.html. Scroll down the page for excellent tips and pictures.

If you want something quick, simple and usable, a company makes a ready-made version, simply a toilet seat that fits a standard five-gallon plastic bucket. Search "Luggable Loo" on the Internet and several places to purchase it will pop up. The basic seat is about $10; with a compatible bucket, it's $15.

Our log-end toilet. "Artistic license," Bruce had said, and delivered one of the world's most beautiful rustic toilets. He had found a 22-inch-diameter partially hollow cedar log, and cut a 16-inch "log-end" from it. With his chainsaw, Bruce carved a section out of the log's center large enough to hold a standard five-gallon plastic bucket. See Figure 8.5. Then he fitted a wooden toilet seat to it, by way of an intermediate piece of plywood, seen in Figure 8.6. With the seat down, the toilet is a whimsical yet functional architectural addition to Stoneview. See Figure 8.7.

Fig. 8.6: *The seat is open, showing the plywood and a nicely fitted transitional flange made from the top of a stainless steel bowl.*

Figure 8.7: *When the seat is closed, the log-end toilet is an attractive and serendipitous feature at Stoneview.*

Nothing at Earthwood puts a smile on a visitor's face like the toilet at Stoneview. Thanks, Bruce!

Electric System

Earthwood is off the grid, so we have a finite amount of power to work with. We decided that kerosene or gas lights are problematic for use with guests who may not be familiar with them. As Stoneview is used less than 30 days of the year (mostly in the summer, when Earthwood's photovoltaic system produces more power than we need), it made more sense to run an electric line out to the guesthouse than to install a separate photovoltaic system.

Most Americans take electricity for granted, thinking that there is always as much as they want available. Just plug in. With an off-the-grid system, one needs to be careful about consumption. We decided to *not* wire any duplex receptacles (plugs) into Stoneview's electrical system, so that people would not be tempted to plug in things like hair dryers, electric grills, or other high-draw appliances. We let guests know in advance that electric lights are available and that's it. There are four 13-watt fluorescent electric lights hard-wired into Stoneview, each with its own wall switch. These bulbs provide the lumens of an ordinary 60-watt incandescent bulb.

Most of the wiring is hidden in the internal framed walls that separate the bathroom from the great room, but there is one piece of Romex tucked up behind a rafter to feed the light fixture over the dining table. This wiring would need to be sheathed in conduit or surface-mounted Wiremold™ if we were connected to the national grid. If your building is to be "on line," the wiring will have to meet code. Get advice from a qualified installation electrician.

"Staining" the Concrete Floor

We now come to a topic where we must report mixed results: the floor stain. Our intent had always been to apply a deep "etching stain" to the floor, the kind of floor that you see at modern airport terminals. However, when we researched etching stains, we discovered that they could not be legally sold in New York and several other states. Further research hinted at some reasons that included possible health dangers during application and the possibility of fumes "eating" nearby masonry. Well, we had a lot of nearby masonry. We could have gone over to Vermont, an hour away, and bought the etching stain, but, frankly, we had become apprehensive about its use. We decided on a more conventional concrete floor "stain." (I use the inverted commas because the stuff is really more of a paint than a stain.)

Cleaning and etching the floor. We asked for concrete floor stain at our supplier. We selected Premium™ Satin Latex Porch and Floor coating, a golden yellow color, coded Rapture 3321. Note that it calls itself a "coating," neither paint nor stain. Following the instructions on the can, we cleaned (etched) the entire concrete floor "to the roughness of 100 grit sandpaper." A six to eight percent solution of muriatic acid (92 to 94 percent water) accomplished this quite nicely. "If acid reacts by bubbling when applied," quoth the instructions, "the solution is strong enough." Rubber gloves and plastic safety glasses are recommended. I got a headache from using the acid. (Open all

Fig. 8.8: *The author etches the concrete floor with muriatic acid.*

the windows, and don't work too long in poorly ventilated spaces.) I washed the floor with the acid mixture, using a plastic bristle brush, let the acid work for five minutes, and then rinsed the floor with clean water. I also cleaned any mortar off the slates with sandpaper and the acid solution, although this was pretty much limited to the slates near the cordwood wall.

I'd been using muriatic acid to clean masonry work for over 20 years, but a fresh reading of the container reveals: "Muriatic Acid and its fumes are destructive to metal, wood, masonry, fabrics, vegetation and many other materials." This warning is very similar to what we had read about etching stains. More in a moment.

Slate sealer. We've been making beautiful floors out of recycled roofing slates at Earthwood since 1982, always sealed with Trewax® Stone and Tile Sealer Finish. When the Stoneview floor was dry, we applied two coats of the sealer to the slates with foam brushes, allowing the slates to dry between coats. We were careful to keep the sealer off the concrete floor, so as not to

Fig. 8.9: *Jaki applies Stone and Tile Sealer to the slates.*

neutralize the etching. The slates can be maintained by applying a single coat of the same sealer every three years. The sealer brings the color out of the slates, gives them depth, and makes them easier to clean.

The floor "stain" or coating. The first coat is thinned with a small amount of water at the rate of a half-pint (one cup) per gallon of coating. We used trim brushes to trim out near the slates and walls, and a four-inch bristle brush to apply the coating. A roller also works fine, once the trim is done. The latex coating dries pretty quickly, but, following recommendations, we let a full 24 hours go by before applying the second uncut finish coat.

We like the look of the floor, even if it is a little more yellow than the sample cards at the store suggested. If you look very closely, you can see some of the polypropylene concrete reinforcing fibers below the coating, but, as we were looking for a leather-like texture, the rough hand-troweled appearance — and the little fibers — do not detract. Now, after two years' use, I think the floor would benefit from a washing and a third coat.

But back to the etching stain. A year after coating the Stoneview floor, Jaki and I visited the beautiful cordwood home of Pat and Wilbur, former students in Wisconsin. Their concrete floor (with in-floor heating, by the way) had been professionally power-troweled. Pat, too, wanted a floor finished with "etching stain," sold legally in Wisconsin. She did all the work herself, following manufacturer's instructions and ended up with a deep, beautiful, easy-to-clean floor. Jaki and I were green with envy. It was what we had wanted from the start, but we were put off by legalities and warnings. Pat just laughed when we told her that we were worried about

Fig. 8.10: *The stained concrete floor is bright and cheerful.*

the fumes eating the mortar… and she didn't get any headaches, either. If faced with the same decision again, we would probably go over to Vermont and sneak back with etching stain. Whether or not it would be as nice on our rougher hand-troweled floor, I cannot say. What we did is more than acceptable, and the floor helps brighten the interior. The choice is yours.

Conclusions

Performance

As I write, we have hosted students and guests at Stoneview over the past two years. Jaki and I have stayed there ourselves. Hundreds of other people have visited the building. When we showed it to one of our neighbors, she said, "I want one of these!"

Based on guests' suggestions and experiences, we tweaked the plumbing and electric systems to the way that they are described in this book. One family of four loved staying at Stoneview, but didn't like the humanure toilet; I don't think they used enough sawdust to absorb all the urine. We do encourage men, after dark at least, to use the great outdoors to lessen the liquid content of the bucket. Yet Joe Jenkins says this is unnecessary if you use enough sawdust.

Everyone likes waking up to a bright cheerful space, made even brighter and more cheerful by the use of colorful bottle-ends and, yes, the bright yellow floor. While in the Dominican Republic, Jaki and I found a Taino-inspired painting that picks up the color scheme and octagonal geometry of Stoneview, and it can be seen in the sleeping area view of Figure 9.1.

Most guests stay during our workshop season, May through September. The earth roof, the shady area, and the mass of the building (floor and walls) all contribute to steady comfortable temperatures in summer. The screened windows all open for cross-ventilation. If we are expecting guests in the late fall,

we will fire up the woodstove early in the morning to bring the mass fabric temperature up to speed for later afternoon use. In the winter, when the building has not been used for weeks, and has gone cold, it is necessary to increase the mass temperature the day *before* the building is to be occupied. We do this by feeding the woodstove every few hours and we can also give a valuable boost by using a space heater that fastens to the top of a five-gallon propane tank, the kind used with gas barbeques.

Winter use. In wintertime, we close off the large window opening that faces in a slightly north-of-east direction, because this window has no solar gain and lots of heat loss. We have a piece of half-inch Celotex™-type rigid insulation that friction-fits right into the opening. See Figure 9.2. The foam has an insulative value of R-4, but, more importantly, the shiny reflective inner surface sends the stove's radiant heat straight back into the room, where it is absorbed by the cordwood masonry and other parts of the building's mass fabric.

Fig. 9.1: *The main sleeping area. The painting picks up the colors and architecture of the building.*

Without this fitted piece, a large part of the stove's heat is radiated right out the window glass. We notice a huge comfort difference the moment we install the fitted piece. The other windows gain solar energy in the winter and lose heat at night, but the little woodstove can keep up with the heat loss. Window quilts, closed at night in the winter, would cut back a great deal on heat loss. We use them at Earthwood. The south-facing windows let in a lot of winter light, because the sun is low in the sky and the sun's rays penetrate deep into the building. Stoneview is as bright in the winter as in the summer, even with one window closed off, but it is bright for a much shorter part of the day. The door, facing west, also lets in late afternoon light. All windows, and the mostly glass door, have privacy shades that can be raised or lowered as desired.

General Use

I have likened the building's use to a hotel room. A futon folds out to make a double bed, and another full-sized bed

Fig. 9.2: *The window with the greatest heat loss is fitted with a reflective insulated panel for wintertime use. Without this panel, the woodstove radiates a lot of heat right out through the window glass.*

sleeps two. Two friendly couples or a family of four can stay at Stoneview, although it is most often occupied by one or two guests. There are no kitchen facilities, but guests eat non-cooked meals at the large rustic slab table that I made about 30 years ago. A kettle of hot water can be kept on the stove in the winter for making coffee, tea or soup. Toast can be made on the stove when a fire is in. If the reader needs a guesthouse for just two people (in one bed), there would be room for a kitchen area. Our floor plan works for our needs, but there are other ways of using the space: a home business, perhaps, or a studio.

Stoneview Cost Details

[2 loads] sand at $65 (for the pad)	130.00
Backhoe (site preparation, spreading sand) 7 hours at $55/hour	385.00
Hired power compactor	45.00
Cast iron hand tamper with handle	34.75
[16] reinforcing bar ½" x 10' @ 3.84	61.44
[61 sheets] 2x8x1" Styrofoam® @ 5.29	322.69
[2] forged bow rakes for drawing concrete	36.79
2" plumbing pipe, fittings and glue	30.06
[4 cubic yards] concrete with fiber mesh, delivered	343.20
[8] 8x8x8'5" girts	357.33
[26] 4x8s, including all rafters, window framing, etc.	735.98
[4 pieces] 2x8x10' cedar	70.00
[112 pieces] 2x6x10' select spruce V-joint T&G planking	548.80
[4] recycled Andersen double-hung windows	175.00
Additional 2x8x12' pine	15.55
[10 sheets] 4x8x½" Sheetrock	91.56
Interior pre-hung door unit	39.00
[20] 2x4x8' studs @ 2.75	55.00
Washed masonry sand, including delivery	117.23

Cost Analysis

The cost analysis is based upon actual receipts, except for a couple of items that were estimated for lack of receipts.

If we round this out to $5,000, I'm confident that we're within $100 (2 percent) of the truth. An assessor, using outside dimensions, would come up with 327 square feet for Stoneview's area, so we built the guesthouse for a materials cost of $15.29 per square foot. There was no labor cost outside of that which was part of heavy equipment contracting (backhoe and dump

[2 bags] mortar mix @ 4.42	8.84
[8 bags] Portland cement @ 7.86	62.88
[13 bags] Type S builders lime @ 6.52	84.76
[50 feet] 8" aluminum flashing	23.00
Cedar shingles	18.75
[2 rolls] Bituthene™ 4000 membrane @ 149.41	298.82
Hardware and miscellaneous	176.40
Topsoil	100.00
[8] 4x4x10' pressure treated roof retaining timbers	72.00
Crushed stone	8.32
Floor coating, slate sealer, caulking, other painting supplies	93.36
Coat rack	21.52
Electrical wiring, parts, switches, lamps, etc.	40.93
Overhead light	26.70
Zodi shower unit	101.00
Sales tax on items above where sales tax is not included	215.86
Estimate for chainsaw & truck fuel and unrecorded odds & ends	50.00
Cordwood: Free, except for fuel recorded in the previous line	0
Total out-of-pocket materials cost, including contracting	$ 4,997.52

truck.) Cost-wise, the reader might do better or worse than us. Final cost depends on what bells and whistles you include, and how skilled you are at making use of indigenous and scrounged materials. But, now, in 2007, two years later, I'm sure that a structural materials cost of less than $20 per square foot is still very doable in rural areas. This figure would not include a well or septic system, each of which might equal the cost of the guesthouse.

Sedum plants and drainage matting were donated to the project, with a combined estimated value of $500. If we include this value to materials cost, we get $5,500, still just $16.82 per square foot.

Furnishings

We already had the futon, table, nightstand, bathroom window and stovepipe. Friends gave us the woodstove, exterior door, bathroom cabinet and sink. We spent:

Three chairs	48.49
Metal bed frame	32.34
Mattress & box spring	134.69
Chest of drawers	70.04
Shower curtain	7.50
Window shades, estimated	35.00
Total for furnishings	$ 328.06

New Outside Stairway

For a couple of years, we made use of a temporary stairway unit to get on the roof. Finally, in December of 2006, I built a good solid outdoor stairs out of 2-by-8 pressure-treated lumber and included a safety handrail. I had to, as so many people wanted to go up and look at the sedum-covered roof. I anchored the base of the steps to a landing made of a single 1,500-pound sandstone slab, using leaded expansion shields and lag screws. The stairs added $50 to the project cost.

Time Analysis

We weren't in a hurry to build Stoneview. It served as a venue for four workshops. Unlike the cost analysis, we did not keep accurate records of the time (man and woman-hours) that was spent on building Stoneview, but I'll make an educated guess. We went at the first phase of the project (tree clearing and footings prep) fairly methodically. I put in a couple of part-time weeks at this and intern Nick Brown put in a full week. The pour itself took about an hour with six people working. Jaki, Nick and I then spent about nine hours between us on slate setting, hand-troweling and pointing between the slates.

Fig. 9.3: *The new stairs provide safe access to the living roof.*

The timber framing and most of the cordwood masonry took place over the course of four three-day workshops, with hands-on work comprising half of each day, the rest being classroom instruction. We did not approach the project as a dire necessity, something that had to be finished quickly. We already had a home for ourselves and two other guesthouses for students. Rather, Stoneview provided a convenient project for workshops and for interns, and so, for a year or so, very little got done between workshops. Then, after the cordwood workshops had taken the walls just about up to the girts:

Darin, Jaki and I completed the snowblocking and the roof.

Intern Dean Koyanagi did internal wall framing, window and door trim, and the like.

Joe Young put in about ten hours on sheetrock, and Bruce Kilgore about the same on the roof.

Cutting trees, dragging brush:	20 hours
Working with heavy equipment operators:	7 hours
Tamping:	4 hours
Other site work, pad prep, prep for pour:	36 hours
The pour:	15 hours
Timber framing:	60 hours
Roof planking, membrane, insulation:	80 hours
Cordwood masonry and snowblocking:	150 hours
Putting soil on roof, retaining timbers:	20 hours
Floor preparation and staining:	20 hours
Internal framing and sheetrocking:	60 hours
Interior wall taping and painting:	20 hours
Plumbing and electric:	30 hours
Outside stairway:	16 hours
Other (materials handling, procurement, etc.)	40 hours
	578 total person-hours

Jaki and I — but mostly Jaki — put in a lot of time on planting and weeding the roof.

And I built the stairway.

A rough estimate of total person-hours appears above, in the sidebar. Workshop man-hours are figured at one-fifth of the time spent, as there is instruction and standing around going on all the time. In other words, Jaki and I, working together, could get as much done in a solid eight-hour day as ten inexperienced students. (Working alone, I can do 24 square feet of completed cordwood in an eight-hour day. There are 244 square feet of cordwood wall at Stoneview, plus snowblocking.)

Intern man-hours are considered at full value. Nick and Dean were each as productive as Jaki or myself.

Let's say 600. As most projects benefit from two people working on them at once, I'd say that Jaki and I could have built Stoneview in 300 hours, just going at it, or about seven and a half five-day (40-hour) weeks. This estimate rings true to me.

Conclusion

Stoneview has met or exceeded all of our goals for it, as outlined in the Introduction and in Chapter 1. We learned a great deal about octagons, octagon corners and the lightweight living roof. Outside of — perhaps — trying the etching stain on the floor, Jaki and I can think of nothing that we would do differently. I know this because I asked her just before writing the previous sentence.

Appendix A:
Annotated Bibliography

Chappell, Steve. *A Timber Framer's Workshop*. Fox Maple Press, Inc., 1999. Distributed by Chelsea Green Publishing Company. ISBN: 1-889269-00-X
Describes the tools, structural considerations, design, roof framing and all the joinery details for traditional wooden-jointed timber framing.

Fine Homebuilding Editors. *Foundations and Concrete Work*. Taunton Press, 1998. ISBN: 1-56158-330-8. Out of print.
There are over 20 good articles in this work, including an excellent one on the floating slab, also called the slab-on-grade foundation. (Be careful: A newer book from Taunton with a similar title, but different ISBN number, does not have the same articles. Look for "The Best of Fine Homebuilding" title head.)

Jenkins, Joseph. *The Humanure Handbook: A Guide to Composting Human Manure*. (3rd Edition.) Joseph Jenkins, Inc., 2005. Distributed by Chelsea Green Publishing. ISBN: 978-0-9644258-3-5.
This is simply the most thorough volume on sensible human waste disposal, and entertainingly written. Stoneview makes use of Joe's simple system.

Nash, George. *Do-It-Yourself Housebuilding*. Sterling Publishing, 1995. ISBN: 0-8069-0424-0.
This huge well-written volume is the one book you need to answer virtually all questions on conventional building, including foundations, electric, plumbing, framing, roofing.

Roy, Rob. *Complete Book of Cordwood Masonry Housebuilding: the Earthwood Method*. Sterling Publishing, 1992. ISBN: 0-8069-8590-9. Out of print.
Covers cordwood masonry, the floating slab foundation, the post-and-beam sauna, and the step-by-step construction of the Earthwood house and out-buildings.

Roy, Rob. *Complete Cordwood DVD*. Earthwood Building School and Chevalier-Thurling Productions, distributed by New Society Publishers. ISBN: 097892570X.
This 195-minute DVD is mostly instructional footage of how to build with cordwood, filmed at Earthwood, but also has a 70-minute tour of a variety of cordwood homes. Indexed for easy viewing.

Roy, Rob. *Cordwood Building: The State of the Art*. New Society Publishers, 2003. ISBN: 0-86571-475-4.
With comprehensive information about cordwood masonry by over 20 of the field's leading proponents, this is a good companion guide to the present work for anyone seeking additional information on the subject.

Roy, Rob. *Earth-Sheltered Houses: How to Build an Affordable Underground Home*. New Society Publishers, 2005. ISBN: 0-86571-521-1.
Discusses and illustrates low-cost methods of earth-sheltering the walls of a building, as well as various methods of doing living roofs. A comprehensive source list of appropriate products is included.

Roy, Rob. *Timber Framing for the Rest of Us*. New Society Publishers, 2003. ISBN: 0-86571-508-4.
A detailed look at using commonly available specialty screws and other metal fasteners to construct strong and beautiful timber frame buildings. Structural considerations are covered in detail, as well as timber procurement and making your own timbers.

Appendix B:
Metric Conversions

Here are some handy conversions for measurements:

If you know:	x by:	To Find:	If you know:	x by:	To Find:
Inches	25.4	millimeters	Millimeters	0.039	inches
Inches	2.54	centimeters	Centimeters	0.39	inches
Feet	0.3048	meters	Meters	3.281	feet
Yards	0.9144	meters	Meters	1.094	yards
Miles	1.609	kilometers	Kilometers	0.622	miles
Fluid ounces	28.4	milliliters	Milliliters	0.035	fluid ounces
Gallons	4.546	liters	Liters	0.220	gallons
Ounces	28.350	grams	Grams	0.035	ounces
Pounds	0.4536	kilograms	Kilograms	2.205	pounds
Short tons	0.9072	metric tons	Metric tons	1.102	short tons
Acres	0.4057	hectares	Hectares	2.471	acres
inches^2	6.452	square centimeters	centimeters^2	0.155	square inches
yards^2	0.836	square meters	meters^2	1.196	square yards
yards^3	0.765	cubic meters	meters^3	1.307	cubic yards
miles^2	2.590	square kilometers	kilometers^2	0.386	square miles

Index

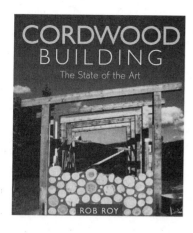

All you need to create beautiful buildings from sawmill left-overs — or even driftwood!

Cordwood Building:
The State of the Art

Rob Roy

Cordwood masonry is an ancient building technique whereby walls are constructed from "log ends" laid transversely in the wall. It is easy, economical, esthetically striking, energy-efficient, and environmentally-sound. *Cordwood Building* collects the wisdom of over 25 of the world's best practitioners, detailing the long history of the method, and demonstrating how to build a cordwood home using the latest and most up-to-date techniques, with a special focus on building code issues.

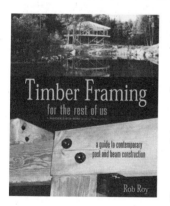

A manual for all without traditional skills who want to build with timber framing.

Timber Framing for the Rest of Us
A Guide to Contemporary Post and Beam Construction

Rob Roy

Timber Framing for the Rest of Us describes the timber framing methods used by most contractors, farmers and owner-builders, methods that use modern metal fasteners, special screws and common sense building principles to accomplish the same goal in much less time. And while there are many good books on traditional timber framing, this is the first to describe in depth these more common fastening methods. The book includes everything an owner-builder needs to know about building strong and beautiful structural frames from heavy timbers, including:

- the historical background of timber framing
- crucial design and structural considerations
- procuring timbers — including different
- foundations, roofs, and in-filling considerations, woods, and recycled materials
- the common fasteners.

A detailed case study of a timber frame project from start to finish completes this practical and comprehensive guide, along with a useful appendix of span tables and a bibliography.

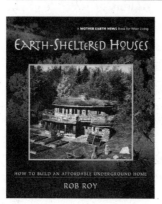

A practical guide for those who want to build their own underground home at a moderate cost.

Earth-Sheltered Houses
How to Build an Affordable Underground Home

Rob Roy

Earth-Sheltered Houses describes the benefits of sheltering a home with earth, and covers all of the construction techniques involved including details on all aspects of construction. Specific methods appropriate for the inexperienced owner-builder are a particular focus. A comprehensive resources section lists all the latest products such as waterproofing membranes, types of rigid insulation and drainage products.

About the Author

Rob Roy has been teaching alternative building methods to owner-builders since 1978, and has become well-known as a writer and educator in fields as disparate as cordwood masonry, earth-sheltered housing, saunas, stone circles and mortgage freedom. This is his thirteenth book for owner-builders. In addition, Rob has created four published videos, also for owner-builders. With his wife Jaki, Rob started Earthwood Building School in 1981. The couple teaches their building techniques all over the world, but their home is at Earthwood in West Chazy, New York. To learn more about Earthwood, visit them online at cordwoodmasonry.com.

If you have enjoyed *Stoneview* you might also enjoy other

BOOKS TO BUILD A NEW SOCIETY

Our books provide positive solutions for people who want to make a difference. We specialize in:

Environment and Justice • Conscientious Commerce • Sustainable Living
Ecological Design and Planning • Natural Building & Appropriate Technology
New Forestry • Educational and Parenting Resources
Nonviolence Progressive Leadership • Resistance and Community

---

New Society Publishers

ENVIRONMENTAL BENEFITS STATEMENT

New Society Publishers has chosen to produce this book on Enviro 100, recycled paper made with **100% post consumer waste**, processed chlorine free and old growth free.

For every 5,000 books printed, New Society saves the following resources:[1]

38	Trees
3,402	Pounds of Solid Waste
3,743	Gallons of Water
4,883	Kilowatt Hours of Electricity
6,185	Pounds of Greenhouse Gases
27	Pounds of HAPs, VOCs and AOX Combined
9	Cubic Yards of Landfill Space

---

[1] Environmental benefits are calculated based on research done by the Environmental Defense Fund and other members of the Paper Task Force who study the environmental impacts of the paper industry.

For more information on this environmental benefits statement, or to inquire about environmentally friendly papers, please contact New Leaf Paper – info@newleafpaper.com Tel: 888 • 989 • 5323.

For a full list of NSP's titles, please call **1-800-567-6772** *or check out our website at:*

www.newsociety.com

NEW SOCIETY PUBLISHERS